What people are saying about

Crayons in the Dryer

Moms will see a bit of themselves and their families in the stories woven throughout *Crayons in the Dryer*. This uplifting pick-up-and-read book is perfect for busy mothers and gently leads the reader to seek and trust God's guidance everyday. Realistic, hopeful, inspiring, and fun, *Crayons in the Dryer* is perfect as a daily devotional for any mom or as a discussion guide for mothers' groups.

ROCHELLE PENNINGTON
SYNDICATED COLUMNIST AND AUTHOR OF
THE GOLDEN FORMULA

I loved this book! I highly recommend it for all the moms out there that need permission to be real; you will enjoy a good laugh and a godly dose of insight and encouragement for daily living.

PATTY ULRICH
HOST, CHRISTIAN FAMILY RADIO, WEMI/WEMY

With been-there-done-that insight, Cheryl Kirking's latest book delivers what busy moms need: encouragement, inspiration, and a healthy dose of laughter. You'll relate to the uplifting real-life stories which will help you find the blessings in everyday life.

WAYNE HOLMES
AUTHOR OF *THE HEART OF A MOTHER* AND
CAUTION: CHILDREN PRAYING

Relaxing with this book is like spending time with your best friend! You can use it as a daily devotional; if you're like me, you won't be able to stop at one story each day! So keep the book close at hand, because you'll want to re-visit this friend again and again.

Readers of *Crayons in the Dryer* will connect with Cheryl's words, just as audiences immediately connect with Cheryl when she speaks. Cheryl shares from the heart; she doesn't claim to be the perfect mother, but she claims God's grace to help her and to bless her everyday. She'll help you find the grace and joy in each day, too!

Crayons in the Dryer will melt your heart! Cheryl's encouraging words remind us of the joys of motherhood, even on hectic days we are up to our ears in sticky kisses.

Crayons
in the Dryer

Crayons in the Dryer

misadventures
and
unexpected blessings
of
Motherhood

CHERYL KIRKING

LIFE JOURNEY®

Bringing Home the Message for Life

COOK COMMUNICATIONS MINISTRIES
Colorado Springs, Colorado • Paris, Ontario
KINGSWAY COMMUNICATIONS LTD
Eastbourne, England

Life Journey® is an imprint of
Cook Communications Ministries, Colorado Springs, CO 80918
Cook Communications, Paris, Ontario
Kingsway Communications, Eastbourne, England

CRAYONS IN THE DRYER
© 2006 by Cheryl Kirking

The Web addresses (URLs) recommended throughout this book are solely offered as a resource to the reader. The citation of these Web sites does not in any way imply an endorsement on the part of the author or the publisher, nor does the author or publisher vouch for their content for the life of this book.

Published in association with the literary agency of Alive Communications, 7680 Goddard St., Ste 200, Colorado Springs, CO 80920.

Cover Design and Photo Illustration: TrueBlue Design/Sandy Flewelling

First Printing, 2006
Printed in the United States of America

1 2 3 4 5 6 7 8 9 10 Printing/Year 10 09 08 07 06

Library of Congress Cataloging-in-Publication Data

Kirking, Cheryl, 1959-
  Crayons in the dryer : misadventures and unexpected blessings of motherhood / by Cheryl Kirking.
     p. cm.
   ISBN 0-7814-4176-5
   1. Motherhood. 2. Mother and child. 3. Motherhood--Religious aspects. I. Title.
HQ759.K553 2005
306.874'3--dc22

                         2005030327

To my mother, Jean Bayles Kirking,
who showed me how to find the blessings in every day

Blessed are the mothers of the earth, for they have combined the practical and the spiritual into the workable way of human life. They have darned little stockings, mended little dresses, washed little faces, and have pointed little eyes to the stars, and little souls to eternal things.
—William L. Stinger

Contents

Acknowledgments

Give thanks to him and praise his name.
For the LORD is good and his love endures for-
    ever;
his faithfulness continues through all genera-
    tions.

                                        —Psalm 100:4–5

My heartfelt thanks ...

To Dave Kilker, my devoted husband of twenty-one
years who encourages my writing and speaking.

To Blake, Bryce, and Sarah Jean, upon whom I practice my mothering skills—you are each a wonderful
blessing, and I am privileged to be your mom.

To Florence Littauer and Marita Littauer, my speaking and writing mentors—your influence has meant
more than you'll ever know.

To my agent, Chip MacGregor of Alive Communications, for finding this book a good home.

To my editor, Mary McNeil, and to Diane Gardner,
assistant editor, for the talent and enthusiasm you both
have invested in this book.

To Cook Communications Ministries. I am grateful to be a part of your publishing team.

To you, dear reader. May you find blessings in every day.

Introduction

> Being a mother, as far as I can tell, is a constant-
> ly evolving process of adapting to the needs of
> your child while also changing and growing as a
> person in your own right.
>
> —Deborah Insel

This book is for real moms with real lives. I hope it helps you to capture some of the everyday, unexpected moments of grace in your life as a mother. This book was inspired by a phone call I received a few years ago.

"Cheryl, you don't know me but my name is Maureen," the woman said. "I heard you speak Saturday at the women's conference in Dubuque."

"Hi, Maureen," I answered, hoping she wasn't selling anything.

"Well, I just wanted to tell you that I really related to what you said about motherhood. You seem so … normal."

"Uh—thank you, I guess."

"I hope you don't take that wrong. You see, my

neighbor dragged me to see you, and I was expecting, you know, 'Little Missus Perfect' to get up and tell me how to be a perfect mother, just like her. But instead you got up there and you are so *far* from perfect!"

It was the emphasis on the word "far" that really warmed my heart.

She continued. "Well, I just wanted to tell you that."

"That I'm so far from perfect?" I laughed.

"Well, yes! I could so-o-o relate to you, especially when you talked about how you have to invite company over in order to get your house cleaned. It was just great." The unmistakable wail of a young child could be heard in the background. "Oh! I have to go. So anyway, thanks so much—you really inspired me!"

I didn't quite know how to interpret that call. I guess I was hoping for some words of praise—a compliment or two would have been nice. But what the caller most liked about me was that I was "pretty normal," and so very far from perfect. I pondered that for a moment and realized Maureen had summed up what we women and mothers need. We need to relate to other women who are living real lives filled with hormones and headaches, delights and delusions, joys and juggling. And we need to understand that "good mother" is a relative term. There's no "one size fits all" formula for good mothering, because every family is a set of unique individuals and circumstances.

Each day blesses us with an opportunity to learn and grow as mothers. Are you developing greater patience? Rediscovering your childlike spirit through the eyes of your children? Have you heightened your ability to let go of small irritations and found humor in everyday nuisances?

I hope this book will help us each find unexpected, everyday blessings in our lives. Whether over morning coffee, in the car waiting to pick up kids from soccer practice, or at day's end, join me as we celebrate our blessed moments as mothers.

> I love little children, and it is not a slight thing
> when they, who are fresh from God, love us.
>   —Charles Dickens

CHAPTER 1

Mom, You're Incomparable!

Part of the art of living is knowing how to compare yourself with the right people.
Dissatisfaction is often the result of unsuitable comparison.

—Dr. Heinrich Sobotka

From the moment a woman learns she's going to have a baby, she begins to dream how motherhood will be. Our early visions are often a little out of focus, like the airbrushed photos of mother and child we see in magazine ads for baby-care products. We're tempted to compare our experiences to those "ideal" mothers that exist only in the glossy pages. Or, we may compare ourselves to other mothers, not realizing they, too, have their limitations and trials.

"I've never been one to compare myself to others," my friend Natalie said. "But since having Alex, it seems like I'm comparing myself to other mothers all the time to see if I measure up. I hate it, but I do it, and it always leaves me feeling so inept."

Her remarks surprised me, as Natalie is the kind of woman many of us wish to be. She left a well-paying job in marketing to stay at home with her son, now two. She's slim and confident and has already established a part-time consulting business she operates from her home.

If Natalie feels insecure, what hope is there for the rest of us? I wondered.

Can you relate to this scenario? Do you find yourself engaging in self-defeating behavior by comparing yourself to others?

I fought falling into this unproductive habit almost as soon as I became pregnant. My friend Cindy was just a month ahead of me in her pregnancy, and we'd looked forward to experiencing our first pregnancies together. We planned to share maternity clothes and take Pregnant Mama Aerobics classes.

We soon learned that our pregnancy experiences would differ dramatically. For one thing, Cindy was carrying one baby. I was carrying three.

Cindy, who is lovely even on a bad-hair day, was even prettier during pregnancy. I, on the other hand, felt miserable. Really, really miserable. I was nauseated all day, every day, from the third week until delivery. Just thinking about food made me physically ill. Although my husband did all the grocery shopping, just trying to write a grocery list for him sent me running to the bathroom. It was bad. And the heartburn! It, too, was constant. By my fifth month, I was already full-term size. My tummy was stretched so taut that it felt like it was on fire, like a bad sunburn, and actually shone like a polished apple. My ribs felt like they would break. How could I possibly grow any more?

Our early visions of motherhood are often a little out of focus, like the airbrushed photos of mother and child we see in magazine ads for baby-care products.

By the fifth month, I was on total bed rest and wasn't feeling very gracious when Cindy stopped by one day to visit. She was absolutely glowing as she told me all about the exercise classes she'd been going to, the ones we'd planned to attend together.

"Well, I guess I have to accept the fact that I can only wear maternity clothes now. I'm getting so big!"

She sighed, patting her little round tummy. She looked so cute in her maternity dress, her hair pulled back with a hair band.

I confess I was a bit envious, since I never even got the chance to wear most of my maternity clothes. I grew so fast, I went directly to men's extra-extra-large sweatpants. Besides, there was little reason to get dressed, since I wasn't allowed out of bed.

"I brought you some of this lotion to prevent stretch marks. So far, it seems to be working for me," Cindy said.

"Thanks. That was thoughtful of you," I said. But I was thinking: *Ha! A little late! I already have stretch marks around the full circumference of my body.*

Cindy's skin was rosy and her eyes shone. "Don't you love being pregnant, Cheryl? It's like you just come alive! You're so aware of your surroundings—music sounds more beautiful, flowers smell sweeter. I know the hormones make me more emotional, but I think it's a good thing—I get all misty eyed and sentimental over the littlest things. Like today, when I was sewing the baby quilt, I got a lump in my throat about becoming a mom."

Cindy was right. I *was* more aware of my surroundings. Right now, in fact, I was feeling pretty emotional. Not exactly lump-in-my-throat emotional—I felt more of a gagging sensation.

"Even food tastes better, don't you think?" Cindy said. "Speaking of food, I've been reading *What to Eat When You're Expecting*, and it says we're supposed to eat eggs every day, for the protein. So I brought you some egg salad sandwiches."

A wave of nausea rolled over me as she presented the sandwiches. Fortunately, I overcame the urge to slap the plate out of her hands and forced what I hoped was a pleasant smile. Cindy is a caring, sweet person, and I knew her thoughtful gestures came from a sincere desire to cheer me. And I was glad she was enjoying her pregnancy—really I was.

"Isn't it fun planning the nursery?" she bubbled. "I'm going with a teddy bear theme, with balloons in primary colors. I've got the room wallpapered and the comforter and curtains made. But I still have to stencil balloons on the crib and changing table. Oh, and I hope to find lamps to match—if I can't find any, I guess I'll just have to try to decorate some lampshades somehow. What theme will your nursery have?"

Theme?! I wanted to scream. *I've had my head in the toilet for five months, I'm stuck here on bed rest, unable to begin preparing the nursery for—not one, but three babies—and now you tell me I'm supposed to have a theme?!* I instead smiled wanly and murmured, "We haven't really decided on a theme yet."

After Cindy left, I groaned. She'd brought me a gift bag of potpourri, and the heady scent made me reel with nausea. I threw it across the room and wondered aloud, "Lord, how am I ever going to get ready for all these babies?"

Then I thought of the perfect nursery theme and laughed in spite of myself. *There was an old woman who lived in a shoe....* With this as the nursery theme, I'd be reminded of that poor old woman who "had so many children she didn't know what to do," and my life would seem easy by comparison!

SET YOUR MINDS ON THINGS ABOVE,

NOT ON EARTHLY THINGS.

COLOSSIANS 3:2

Dear God, may I strive to meet your standards for a good mother, not someone else's.

CHAPTER 2

Watching the Fish Eat

When a woman tells the truth she is creating the possibility for more truth around her.

—Adrienne Rich

I did something daring today. I said no without offering an "acceptable" excuse. I was at a meeting where I was asked to serve on a committee that would require many Thursday evening meetings. And I said no.

I said it politely, graciously. But the others around the conference table just looked at me, waiting. Three long seconds ... four ... five. Waiting, waiting, waiting for my important excuse. They couldn't move on until I had explained my no.

"I want to be home to tuck the kids in at night," I said. Most people around the table nodded in understanding.

I did something daring today. I said no without offering an "acceptable" excuse.

"We can make sure we're done by eight thirty, so you can be home in time to tuck the kids in," the chairperson said. The others waited for me to agree.

"Well, um, that's right when we're watching the fish eat," I explained. "After I've quizzed the children for Friday's spelling tests, we watch the fish. It's an important time in our family's week. It seems to set the tone for the next day, and when I'm gone on Thursday nights, Friday just doesn't go as well."

My words sounded almost silly as they tumbled out. No one said, "Oh, of course, Cheryl, we understand."

I could have added, "I've got a book manuscript due to the publisher in two months that I've got to work on." That would have been a sufficiently important excuse. After all, that's my career. They would have accepted my answer and moved on.

But the truth is, I'm not writing on Thursday evenings. I'm being Mom. I'm reviewing spelling words for Friday's test. I'm checking math answers. I'm making sure permission notes are signed, book reports written, weekly assignments completed. And when schoolwork is done and the children have brushed their teeth and gotten their PJs on, we gather on the couch in front of the aquarium to watch the fish eat.

This is when I hear about Blake's plans to be a paleontologist. It's when I learn how Bryce handled the bully on the playground. This is when Sarah Jean explains she doesn't want to wear bows in her hair anymore because "none of the other girls do, Mama."

The committee members were still looking at me. Feeling guilty, I almost said, "Okay, I'll do it." But I didn't. I didn't because my reason for saying no is important.

We have to watch the fish eat.

FOR EVERYTHING THERE IS A SEASON,
AND A TIME FOR EVERY MATTER UNDER HEAVEN.
ECCLESIASTES 3:1 ESV

Lord, there are so many places I need to be!
Help me know when to say yes and
when to say no.

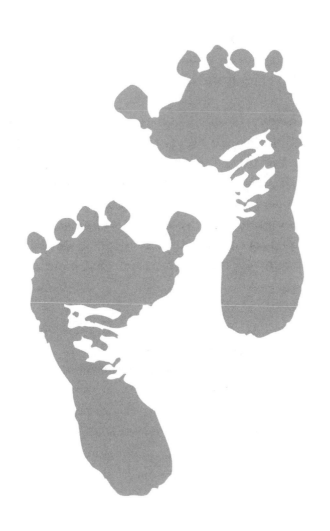

CHAPTER 3

A Child's Wisdom

A time of quietude brings things into proportion
and gives us strength.

—Gladys Taber

A few years ago, we decided to give my father a surprise birthday party. Four-year-old Bryce was especially excited about the party for his grandpa. He spent all day making streamers and paper hats and decorating the house. He instructed his brother and sister as to where they should hide and how to yell "Surprise!" with the proper inflection and zeal.

Finally Grandpa made his long-awaited appearance, and Bryce led the troops in the noisy revelry. But, as so often happens in life, reality failed to measure up to his great expectations. The party horns weren't tooting properly; the guests weren't enthusiastic enough;

Sometimes the best thing is to not do, to wait a while. Be still. Let things settle back into perspective.

and the cake, under the pink frosting, was just plain white—not chocolate. Finally, Bryce could take no more disappointment and melted into a sobbing little heap on the floor. Scooping him up in my arms, I took him to a quiet room where he poured out his troubles.

"Sweetheart, what can we do to help you feel better?" I asked, as he flopped across my lap.

"Mommy," he cried, "can we rewind the party?"

"Honey, I wish we could, but we can't rewind time," I answered, smoothing his hair from his damp forehead. "But we can start from right now and find a way to make the rest of the day better."

"Well," he sniffled, "maybe we could just hit 'pause' a little while before we go back, okay?"

"That's a good idea," I said.

As I rocked my little boy, smelling his sweet hair and feeling him relax, I realized I'd learned two important lessons from him. For one thing, the kid was watching way too many videos!

More important, my wise little boy reminded me that sometimes, when life is overwhelming, the best thing to do is to just "hit pause" for a little while.

BE STILL, AND KNOW THAT I AM GOD.

PSALM 46:10

COME TO ME, ALL YOU WHO ARE WEARY AND

BURDENED, AND I WILL GIVE YOU REST.

MATTHEW 11:28

Lord, grant me perspective when I'm overwhelmed and help me show my children the value of being still and finding comfort in knowing you are God.

CHAPTER 4

Learning as You Go

More than any other human relationship, over-
whelmingly more, motherhood means being
instantly interruptible, responsive, responsible.

—Tillie Olson

Mommy, don't wipe off my kiss," Sarah Jean
chastised me after a particularly juicy smooch
on my cheek.

"I wasn't wiping it off, I was rubbing it in," I
answered.

I was glad I had a ready response, thanks to a
Family Circus comic I'd read years earlier. I don't
remember whether it was little Billy or P.J. or Dolly; but
I do recall one of the cartoon kids had spied his daddy
wiping away a sticky kiss, and the wise father had
explained he was, instead, "rubbing the kiss in."

Mothers need to have such responses at the ready,

When your newborn first squeezes your little finger, he's taken hold of your heart forever.

such as, "Oops, how did that get in there?" when a child finds a piece of artwork that "accidentally" got thrown away.

We learn these handy comebacks and other "tricks of the trade" from our own mothers and from watching others around us. Parenting books can be a valuable resource, but many mothering lessons can be appreciated only through experience. Real-life mothering teaches us that:

- babies prefer spitting up on clean clothes (yours or theirs);
- the world's hardest substance isn't the diamond: it's oatmeal that has dried on the wall;
- it helps to think of stretch marks as badges of honor;
- anyone who claims to know everything about raising kids hasn't had any;
- you must hide the chocolate chips after having kids;

- the fingerprints on the walls get higher each year;
- the toys on kids' Christmas lists tend to get smaller but more expensive each year;
- the smell of microwave popcorn made late at night will wake the kids;
- "long bubble bath" is an oxymoron;
- you consider yourself lucky if you get to leave the conditioner on your hair the full three minutes;
- you rarely get to eat an entire meal hot until your children are at least four years old;
- when your newborn first squeezes your little finger, he's taken hold of your heart forever;
- one of motherhood's most important but difficult lessons is learning to let go.

BEHOLD, CHILDREN ARE A GIFT OF THE LORD.
PSALM 127:3 NASB

Dear God, may I be open to the unexpected lessons and blessings that my children bring me every day.

CHAPTER 5

Glad They're Mine

We worry what a child will be tomorrow, yet we forget that he is someone today.

—Stacia Tauscher

You sure had your kids close together," the woman behind me in line at the post office said, as my preschoolers hugged my knees. "How far apart are they, anyway?"

"Oh, about a minute," I replied.

"So what are they—twins?"

"Triplets."

"Omigosh! Triplets! I'll bet they drive you crazy," she said.

"They're the most fun I've ever had," I answered, hoping to conceal my resentment at her insensitivity. *What nerve*, I thought, *speaking about my children as if they were invisible!*

I want to be sure my children know what blessings they are. It's my job to make sure they know it.

She rolled her eyes. "I'm glad they're yours, not mine!"

"I'm glad too," I said, still smiling.

Have you ever noticed how some people seem to want to throw a wet blanket on your joy? When I was pregnant, I often heard, "This is the easy part—wait till they're born!" Actually, considering I was throwing up around the clock, I doubted it could get worse.

When they were babies, I'd hear, "Yeah, well, it gets harder—just wait until they're walking."

When they were walking, it was, "Just wait until they reach the 'Terrible Twos!'"

When they were two years old, I'd hear, "Wait until they're teenagers."

Mothers of teens hear, "Yeah, well, just wait until they're driving."

I don't usually mind the remarks. I know people are just making conversation, and some folks find it easier to talk about negative things than positive. Like complaining about the weather, it's something to talk about.

Or maybe some people feel they're being empathetic. I've done that. Commiserating with other parents can reassure us we're not alone in our parenting trials. It can be helpful to know other parents experience similar challenges. Yes, children can be challenging. Yes, they're expensive to raise. Yes, they tire us out sometimes.

But I *want* to be sure my children know what blessings they are at every age, every day. It's my job to make sure they know it.

CONSIDER IT ALL JOY, MY BRETHREN, WHEN YOU
ENCOUNTER VARIOUS TRIALS.

JAMES 1:2 NASB

Lord, thank you for my children. May I always know that parenting is a privilege.

CHAPTER 6

The Pencil on My Windowsill

Man must work, that is certain as the sun. But he may work grudgingly or he may work gratefully; he may work as a man or as a machine. There is no work so rude that he may not exalt it; no work so impassive that he may not breathe a soul into it; no work so dull that he may not enliven it.

—Henry Giles

The two halves of a broken pencil sit on the window ledge above my kitchen sink. I placed them there several years ago, along with the seashells, rocks, Play-Doh animals, and other reminders of my children's love for me and mine for them.

Why a broken pencil? Here's the story....

The night I placed the pencil on my windowsill, eight-year-old Blake had homework to do. The assignment was easy enough—write five sentences about what you did today. But he didn't want to do it. He sulked at the kitchen table as I put away supper dishes.

"How come Bryce gets to play outside?"

"Because Bryce doesn't have homework. Now just write a few sentences and be done with it. Then you can play too."

"I don't have anything to write," he mumbled.

"Just write what you did today."

"I didn't do anything."

"Blake, you did lots of things today. You went to school. You called your best friend, James. You caught a frog. You helped make pudding. You had soccer practice. You bugged your sister. That's six sentences already!"

"I don't want to write that."

I didn't argue. He knew what needed to be done. I continued to work in the kitchen.

"I'm so mad.... I feel like breaking this pencil in half!"

I offered no response. But the silence was broken by a *snap!*

Blake gasped, staring at the two jagged pieces of his brother's new Green Bay Packers pencil.

I turned to give him "the look." He was pale; eyes wide. After ten long seconds, I said quietly, "Blake, I'm going for a walk. When I get back, I expect you will have your homework done, your teeth brushed, your pajamas on, and yourself in your bed. We will then have a talk. Understood?"

He nodded. He knows when he's in trouble.

I wanted to smile and tousle his hair, but it would have broken the spell of fear I'd effectively cast. So I left him at the kitchen table, looking pathetic and small, holding the pencil halves.

I enjoyed my evening walk, going a little slower than usual to give Blake time to complete his tasks. I opened the front door loudly upon my return to warn him that Mom was home. As I climbed the stairs to his room, I prayed for wisdom.

He was wearing his dinosaur PJs and was curled up in a little ball on his bed. I slid in next to him and pulled him close.

"You're in for a treat, big guy! Mom's going to tell you a story!"

Blake groaned. My poor children have had to suffer through quite a few of Mom's

Helping my child mature emotionally requires me to assess areas I need to work on in myself as well.

parables. They claim to hate them, but it doesn't stop me.

"Actually," I said, "you're in for a double delight, 'cause I've got *two* stories for you tonight!"

"Oh no," he groaned again, rolling his eyes.

"The first story is about a medium-sized, third-grader kind of boy. He didn't want to do his homework one night because he had to write four sentences and it was just too boring."

"Mom, I did *not* have to write *four* sentences. I had to write *five* sentences."

"Well, I'm not talking about you," I said. "This boy's name was Joe, and he had to write four sentences. Joe was so angry, he felt like breaking the pencil, even though it was his brother's Green Bay Packers pencil. And you know what?" I didn't wait for Blake to answer. "He did! Broke the pencil right into two pieces! Well, do you know what Joe's mother did?"

Blake shook his head.

"She did nothing! She just patted his head and said, 'Poor Joe, you're grumpy and tired, and I know it's hard to do homework.' Well, the next night Joe's little sister was being a pest. She kept putting her Beanie Babies on Joe's head, even when he told her to stop. So he bopped her—WHACK—harder than he meant to, and she screamed and got a big red mark on her arm. And do you know what Joe's mom did?"

"What?" Blake asked, eyes wide.

"Nothing! She just said, 'Joe, I've had quite enough of you for today. Go outside.'"

"You're kidding!" Blake exclaimed. "That's it?"

"Yup. Well, Joe grew up to be an architect. One day his boss said, 'Joe, I need you to make some changes in the designs you drew up yesterday. The client has changed his mind.'

"'What?' Joe bellowed. 'Those designs are perfect. I'm not going to change them. It's stupid and unnecessary and a waste of my time!'

"'Joe,' his boss shouted back, 'we don't need that kind of attitude here. You're fired.'

"Poor Joe. He'd never learned to control his temper. He'd never learned to do things he didn't want to do. And now he was without a job. He was angry and sad.

"Now let me tell you about another third-grader-sized boy. His name was Blake."

"Mom," Blake moaned, "I don't want to be in your story."

"Who said anything about you? It's purely coincidental that this boy's name was Blake. Anyway, one day Blake had to write four sentences for homework. And he didn't want to do it. He said, 'I'm so angry, I'm going to break this pencil!' And he did. Do you know what his mother did?"

"Nothing?" Blake asked hopefully.

"Of course not, because Blake's mother was very wise. She said, 'Blake, I know you're tired and grumpy,

CRAYONS IN THE DRYER

but you still have to finish your homework. And tomorrow when you come home from school, you must empty the dishwasher.'

"'But it's not my turn to empty the dishwasher,' that Blake complained.

"'And it wasn't your pencil that you broke, either,' his mother answered. 'Now would you like to stop complaining and get to work, or would you like to keep complaining and sweep the floor tonight too?'

"And what do you think Blake did?"

"He did his homework," my Blake muttered.

"Indeed he did, and he emptied the dishwasher without whining. For Blake was a very smart boy. Well, he grew up and became a scientist. He worked in a laboratory where he was conducting an experiment to test a new mosquito repellent. One day his boss said, 'Blake, I'm afraid the custodian accidently dumped out your experiment from yesterday. You'll have to redo it.'

"'Well, that's a bummer,' Blake said. But he knew it had to be done, so he did it. And while conducting the experiment the second time, he accidentally made a new discovery and invented a solution that removes the itch from mosquito bites. The discovery made Blake and his company very rich, and people all over the world rejoiced, for they would never have to scratch another mosquito bite again.

"How very smart Blake was to redo the experiment

without complaining. And do you know why he was so smart? Because Blake had a wise and wonderful mother who taught him that it's best to do work without complaining. And his mother also taught Blake there are consequences to actions. How very lucky Blake was that his mother made him empty the dishwasher even though it wasn't his turn!

"Now wasn't that a great story?" I asked as I pulled Blake close and smooched his cheek.

He vigorously wiped his cheek with the back of his hand and sighed. "Are you done?"

"Yup, unless you'd like to hear another story?"

"No thanks."

"You sure?"

"Believe me, I'm sure!"

And that's why there's a broken pencil on my kitchen window ledge. Thanks to my son, I have this little reminder to prompt me to approach my daily tasks with joy.

SHE ... WORKS WITH EAGER HANDS.

PROVERBS 31:13

Lord, I, too, often whine when there's a task to be done that I don't want to do. Help me to approach my work with a positive attitude.

49

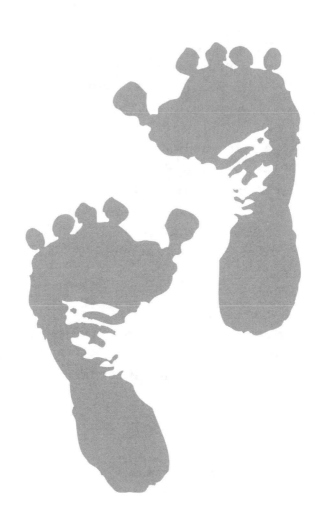

CHAPTER 7

A Mother's Heart Is a Child's Classroom

What a mother sings to the cradle goes all the way down to the coffin.

A mother's heart is a child's schoolroom.
—Henry Ward Beecher

Mommy."

I opened my eyes a crack to see a single, huge, blue eye peering at me. It wasn't Cyclops; it was three-year-old Blake, his nose pressed against mine, causing me to go cross-eyed.

"Mommy," Blake repeated, crawling up onto my stomach, "why are you lying on the couch?"

I tried to sit up, but dropped back onto the pillow. My head throbbed. My body ached. My throat was on fire. The flu that had traveled through the family had finally hit me.

"Oh, sweetie," I groaned. "Mommy's not feeling so good. I think that ol' flu bug that bit you last week decided to bite me today."

"The flu bug bit Mommy!" Blake announced, sliding off the couch. "The flu bug bit Mommy!"

Three concerned doctors immediately came to my side. Sarah Jean put her hand on my forehead and comforted me. "It's okay, sweetheart," she cooed. "You'll feel better soon. Would you like a juice box?"

Kindness isn't taught; it's caught— kind of like the flu.

All three scampered off. Soon Sarah Jean returned with the juice box. "Can you put the straw in by yourself or would you like me to do it?"

Bryce returned with "Tickley," his pale-green blanket. "I'll tuck you in all comfy-cozy," he said soothingly, tucking Tickley up under my chin. Oh, it felt soft!

Blake ran upstairs to the bedroom and returned with his blanket and added another layer of coziness, as well as a sweet smooch on my forehead.

It felt nice to be tucked in.

"Thank you, sweeties," I said. "You're taking such good care of Mommy. I'm feeling a little better already."

And I did. It felt good to rest. The past week had been challenging, with three flu-ridden children and me trying to fight off the virus. I'd been experiencing pangs of guilt: My house was in disarray, dishes were piled high in the sink, laundry was left unfolded, I had served canned ravioli twice in two days, and I had been less than sweet tempered toward my husband.

Yet, through it all, I must have done something right. It warmed my heart to realize my children were saying and doing the same things that I'd said and done the past week as I tended to them. It was reassuring to know I must have made them feel loved, because that's just how they were making me feel—loved and "comfy-cozy."

I've heard it said that kindness isn't taught; it's caught—kind of like the flu. The following poem is a reminder of this. A thoughtful friend attached a copy of it to one of my baby-shower gifts, and it has hung on my refrigerator ever since. (I've tried to track the poem's author and have learned that although it has appeared in several magazines and newspapers, the author remains unknown.)

Maybe it was written by a mom who had the flu, whose little ones reminded her that her actions are indeed noticed and imitated.

By a Child

When you thought I wasn't looking,
I saw you hang my first painting on the refrigerator,
And I immediately wanted to paint another one.

When you thought I wasn't looking,
I saw you feed a stray cat,
And I learned that it was good to be kind to animals.

When you thought I wasn't looking,
I saw you make my favorite cake for me,
And I learned that little things can be the special
    things in life.

When you thought I wasn't looking,
I heard you say a prayer,
And I knew there is a God I could always talk to, and
    I learned to trust in God.

When you thought I wasn't looking,
I saw you make a meal and take it to a friend who
    was sick,
And I learned that we all have to help take care of
    each other.

When you thought I wasn't looking,
I saw you give of your time and money to help
    people who had nothing,
And I learned that those who have something should
    give to those who don't.

When you thought I wasn't looking,
I felt you kiss me good night,
And I felt loved and safe.

When you thought I wasn't looking,
I saw you take care of our house and everyone in it,
And I learned we have to take care of what we are
    given.

When you thought I wasn't looking,
I saw how you handled your responsibilities, even
    when you didn't feel good,
And I learned that I would have to be responsible
    when I grow up.

When you thought I wasn't looking,
I saw tears come from your eyes,
And I learned that sometimes things hurt, but it's all
    right to cry.

When you thought I wasn't looking,
I saw that you cared,
And I wanted to be everything that I could be.

When you thought I wasn't looking,
I learned most of life's lessons that I need to know
To be a good and productive person when I grow up.

When you thought I wasn't looking,
I looked at you and wanted to say,
"Thanks for all the things I saw when you thought I
    wasn't looking."

                                        —Author unknown

TRAIN A CHILD IN THE WAY HE SHOULD GO, AND WHEN HE IS
OLD HE WILL NOT TURN FROM IT.

PROVERBS 22:6

*Lord, Source of all goodness and love, may
your love shine through me upon
my children every day.*

CHAPTER 8

Stop, Look, and Listen

Listen, or your tongue will keep you deaf.
—Native-American proverb

One afternoon, four-year-old Blake sat on the floor beside me, happily bending pipe cleaners into various creations as I plugged away at the computer.

"Look at my invention, Mom," he'd chirp.

"Uh-huh, Blake, that's nice."

Every minute or so, he'd have a new invention for me to admire. "See, Mommy, this one's a windmill."

I briefly turned to look. "That's nice, honey."

He continued to describe all the unique features of his latest invention and finally asked, "Did you hear me, Mom?"

"I'm listening," I said. "Sometimes Mommy does two things at once, but I'm listening."

"But I don't see you hearing me," Blake protested.

That got to me. Bull's-eye. Straight to the heart! How could my son know I was interested in him if he couldn't *see* me listening? Whether we're four or one hundred four, we need to feel validated. We need to know that those we love care about the things that matter to us. We need to hear it—and we need to see it.

Listen to your children as you would have them listen to you.

Years ago, when I taught junior high school, one of my eighth-grade students stopped by my room after school, wanting to discuss some personal matters.

"I think perhaps you need to talk to your mother about this," I said.

"Why?" she asked. "She doesn't know anything about me—she just thinks she does."

Many parents are tempted to throw up their hands in despair, declaring, "I've given up trying to understand that kid." Or, equally damaging, we may think we know our children better than we actually do. Children are in a constant state of change. We need to find out where they are today, which is a different place than they were yesterday or will be tomorrow. Our children need to "see that we're hearing them."

LET THE WISE LISTEN.

PROVERBS 1:5

God, help me to be wise, to be a good listener.
Teach me to hold my tongue and
open my ears.

CHAPTER 9

Cookie Cutters Are for Cookies

Most of us are like snowflakes trying to be like each other, yet knowing full well that no two snowflakes are ever identical. If we were to devote the same amount of energy in trying to discover the true self that lies buried deep within our own nature, we would all work harmoniously with life instead of forever fighting it.
—William E. Elliott

He is such an easy baby because his mother was happy during her pregnancy."

"He was a fussy baby because his mother was tense during her pregnancy."

"She's such a shy child because her older brother is so overbearing."

Have you ever heard similar attempts to explain a child's personality? Environmental circumstances such as birth order and parenting styles certainly play a role in affecting behavior. But my triplets, although raised in the same environment, were born with very different personalities. While we can do a lot to shape our children, we also need to recognize that they come to us not merely to be "molded," but to be "unfolded" to bring out the best in each child's unique personality.

Each child is a unique individual, a miracle that cannot be duplicated. Each is a holy miracle of God.

My triplets were born within minutes of each other and for the early years of their lives shared a bedroom, wore each other's clothes, ate the same food, came into contact with the same people, listened to the same stories and music, and breathed the same air. Because they happened to be part of a four-year medical study of premature babies, evaluations revealed they were also very similar in their physical and cognitive development.

Yet their personality differences delight and sometimes amaze us. While I strive to be consistent and fair, they each have different wants and needs that I have to take into consideration. A cookie-cutter approach to raising kids doesn't work, and it isn't fair to children to try to fit them into the same mold.

For instance, when my kids were four years old, they decorated gingerbread cookies at Christmastime. Three pairs of little hands were washed. Three little aprons were tied around three excited "bakers." I divided the cookies equally and placed dishes of colored frosting, gumdrops, candy sprinkles, and M&Ms on the table, then gave them each three gingerbread men to decorate.

Fun-loving Bryce immediately began slathering frosting with wild abandon, cramming as many candies on his cookies as possible. This bothered Sarah Jean, who likes things more controlled. She began wailing, "Mommy, make him stop! He's using all the candy up. Stop him!" I quickly intervened, dividing the candies equally.

Meanwhile, thoughtful Blake hadn't yet begun his decorating.

"Blakey, how are you going to decorate your cookies?" I asked.

"I don't know yet," he said. Analytical by nature, he needed time to think about it.

"Blake," I said, "you can decorate them any way you want to. There's no right or wrong way to decorate cookies."

"Will you help me get the face right?" he asked.

"Honey, you can do it. There's no right or wrong way to decorate a cookie."

"But I want it right!" he insisted. So I guided his hand with mine and we carefully made the eyes, nose, mouth, and hair.

"Now you decorate the body." And he did, with a single yellow M&M "button," perfectly centered on his gingerbread man.

"Don't you want to put anything more on your cookie?" I asked.

"No," he said. "I want to wipe my hands now so I can go play Legos."

"What about your other two cookies? Don't you want to decorate them?"

"Nope," he answered happily. "I like this one." And off he scampered to his "work" of building with his Legos. After all, he had created his perfect cookie; to make any more would simply be redundant.

"I'll take his candy," Bryce immediately volunteered.

"No, Mommy!" Sarah Jean squawked. "Divide them!"

Three peas in a pod? Hardly.

My children have shown me, as I'm sure yours have shown you, that every child is a unique individual, a miracle that can't be duplicated. Each has been given a separate body, personality, and soul, divinely chosen. Each is a holy miracle of God.

BEFORE I FORMED YOU IN THE WOMB I KNEW YOU.
JEREMIAH 1:5

*Lord, you have lovingly created each one of
your children as a one-of-a-kind masterpiece.
Grant me insight into my child's matchless
personality, so that I may help him
be the best he can be.*

CHAPTER 10

A Bouquet of Bananas

One of the best things you can give children,
next to good habits, are good memories.
—Sydney J. Harris

Look what we bought for you, Mommy!" Four-year-old Bryce excitedly unpacked the groceries he and Daddy had just purchased. "We bought some Cheerios, we bought a can of peaches." He proudly placed each item on the counter. "We bought two loaves of Kleenex. Oh, and look what special thing we bought." He reached into a bag again and exclaimed with a flourish, "We brought you a bouquet of bananas!"

Two loaves of Kleenex and a bouquet of bananas—how cute is that?

I immediately wrote the incident down in a notebook so I wouldn't forget it.

I learned this from my mother. Raising five children on a bustling farm, life was busy, but she managed to capture memories by jotting them down in a notebook she kept handy. Although she didn't get our baby books filled in until we were all grown, she had all the information and memories recorded in the notebooks. Now I keep a couple of spiral notebooks in the living room and in the kitchen, so I can jot down moments I want to remember: lost teeth, cute expressions, first steps, happy thoughts.

Once written, a memory is forever preserved.

Most entries are simple, unexpected moments in our everyday routine. I wrote the following in my notebook when Sarah Jean was just two. She was in her high chair, and I was serving a midafternoon snack.

"Mama, can I have some snowflakes?"

"Some what, sweetheart?"

"Snowflakes," she said.

Unsure what she meant, I asked, "What will you do with the snowflakes?"

"Eat them." She smiled, pointing to her bowl.

Aha! Cornflakes! After a few more questions and answers, it turned out she'd eaten them for the first time at our neighbor's house the day before.

Another memory was made when we went for a walk with the stroller. Her blue eyes sparkled as she tugged on my jacket and whispered, "Mama, I've got watermelons in my pocket!"

"Watermelons?" I asked.

"Yes. See?" She reached into the pocket of her pink fuzzy jacket and triumphantly pulled out a small handful of pussy willows. I have no idea why she called them watermelons, but it was just so cute—worth jotting in the notebook.

At my parenting workshops, I encourage mothers to keep a book just for lovely memories. "Don't worry about neatness," I say. "Use a pencil, crayon, whatever is handy; just get it written down." Once written, a memory is forever preserved.

A young mother at a woman's conference asked me if my kids were exceptionally cute or if I just managed to remember the things they say because I write them down. Well, of course I think my kids are exceptionally cute—don't we all? But I do make an extra effort to record the sweet things they say and do. Someday I'll get them all neatly inscribed in individual journals for each child. In the meantime, the memories are safely captured in writing so they won't fade.

CRAYONS IN THE DRYER

THESE DAYS SHOULD BE REMEMBERED AND
OBSERVED IN EVERY GENERATION.

ESTHER 9:28

*Thank you, God, for the unexpected blessings
you give us, which delight and continue to
remind us of future blessings.*

CHAPTER 11

Holding On

Remember, we all stumble, every one of us.
That's why it's a comfort to go hand in hand.
—Emily Kimbrough

Let's take a piece of pumpkin bread to Gramma Fran," I suggested. "Who wants to go with me?"

Six-year-old Bryce immediately volunteered, always happy to visit with our neighbor at the end of the block.

Bundled in warm coats, mittens, and scarves, we were surprised to find the day's melted snow had formed ice as the evening temperature dropped. Holding hands, we minced our way slowly down the street. I wished we'd put on boots, as our shoes had little traction. The light dusting of snow made the hidden ice especially perilous.

We all need a hand to hold.

Who-o-o-o-o-o-oaaaa! Bryce suddenly lurched as he slipped on a hidden patch of ice. Tightening my grip on Bryce's mittened hand, I struggled to keep him upright and to prevent myself from falling as he pitched forward, then back, then forward again. Amazingly, after several seconds of teetering, I managed to steady him and regain my own balance.

"Whew," Bryce exclaimed. "You almost fell, Mom! It's a good thing I was holding your hand!"

IF THE LORD DELIGHTS IN A MAN'S WAY, HE MAKES HIS STEPS FIRM; THOUGH HE STUMBLE, HE WILL NOT FALL, FOR THE LORD UPHOLDS HIM WITH HIS HAND.

PSALM 37:23–24

Although I wish I could, I can't always hold my child's hand to keep him from falling. Uphold my child, O God! Help me to teach my precious child to cling tightly to your strong, loving hand.

CHAPTER 12

Mommy Says

There was never a child so lovely but his mother
was glad to get him asleep.

—Ralph Waldo Emerson

My niece Megan was just three years old when Grandpa bought a new video camera. Eager to try it out, he was glad the camera was rolling when he captured this delightful exchange:

"Megan, what does the doggy say?" Grandpa asked from behind the camcorder.

Smiling at the camera, Megan beamed and answered, "Woof, woof!"

"And what does the kitty say?" Grandpa asked.

"Meow, meow!"

"And what does the cow say?"

"Moo, moo!" Megan replied.

"And what does Mommy say?"

"GO TO BED!" Megan exclaimed.

What does the mommy say at your house?

SHE SPEAKS WITH WISDOM, AND FAITHFUL
INSTRUCTION IS ON HER TONGUE.

PROVERBS 31:26

*Lord, help me to instruct my children, guide
my children, and love my children as you
would have me to do. Help me be firm when
needed and always loving. It is a holy
privilege to be a mother. Help me use this
privilege wisely.*

CHAPTER 13

Could You Repeat the Question?

How did you come to me, my sweet?
From the land that no one knows.
Did Mr. Stork bring you here on his wings?
Or were you born in the heart of a rose?
I carried you under my heart, my sweet,
And I sheltered you safe from alarms,
'Till one wonderful day, the dear God looked
   down
And my darling lay safe in my arms.
—Olga Petrova
"To a Child That Inquires"

I was loading the dishwasher, when out of the blue Bryce asked me, "How do people get to be mommies?"

"What, honey?" I asked. I wanted to be sure I had heard him correctly.

"How do people get to be mommies?" he repeated. I wasn't expecting this from my kindergartner, but I'd

May my children trust me to answer them honestly.

already given some thought as to how I would answer the inevitable question when it arose. So I began to explain in very simple terms how people get to be mommies.

"No." Bryce shook his head. "Not mamas! How do people get to be mommies?"

"Bryce," I said, "I don't think I understand your question."

"Well, you know how people get wrapped up, all over, in lots and lotsa toilet paper?"

Aha! Mummies! It was October, and he must have seen Halloween pictures of mummies. Whew! Compared to the question I thought he was asking, this was relatively easy to explain.

LET THE WISE LISTEN.

PROVERBS 1:5

Lord, help me to really listen to my children.
Don't let me brush off their questions.
Keep me from making assumptions about
what they're saying.
Help me to take the time to find the meaning
behind their questions.

*Keep me open and available. I know the
questions are going to get tougher.
May my children trust me to answer them
honestly. And when I don't know the answers,
direct me to the resources I need to find them.
You promised to be my Counselor. Thank
you for your Holy Spirit that guides me.
Being a mom is challenging, Lord. I'm up for
the challenge, knowing that you
are guiding me all the way.*

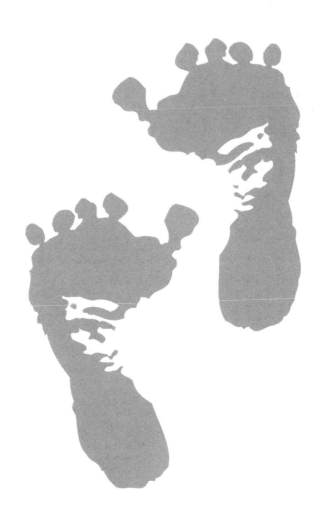

CHAPTER 14

Costume Change

The greatest gifts you can give your children are the roots of responsibility and the wings of independence.

—Denis Waitley

'm going to be something cool this year for Halloween!" announced Bryce.

"Cool?" I asked.

"Yup. In kindergarten the boys hafta have cool costumes," he said. "I want to be a "Powah Wanjah." (Translated: Power Ranger. Bryce still had trouble pronouncing *r*'s.)

He had bought the Power Ranger costume with a dollar of his own at a July garage sale. I saw no harm in buying the costume, and he'd had lots of fun playing in it. But I'd hoped he'd tire of it and want to be something else for Halloween, because I didn't particularly

Motherhood

is a bittersweet

dichotomy.

We lament the

passing of

time, yet

delight in

watching our

children grow.

like the *Power Rangers* TV program. I didn't think it was a good choice for preschoolers.

I once watched about four minutes of an episode, long enough to decide my kids weren't going to be watching the show any time soon. Too much kicking and punching, not enough nurturing and learning. Nevertheless, Bryce knew about the show and thought that a "Powah Wanjah" costume would be "cool."

I wasn't ready for "cool"—I was still hoping for "cute." On his first Halloween, I put bunny ears on him and attached a cotton tail to his little blue sleeper. He was so sweet! For his second Halloween, he was a little gray mouse, complete with pink nose and whiskers. When he was three, I was ready to dress him as a pumpkin, along with his brother and sister, in order to make a pumpkin patch—but he wanted a kitty costume. I presumed he wanted to be a typical black cat, but he wanted to be "a harmless white kitty." Even at three years old, his gentle spirit shone through his costume choice. For his four-year-old preschool party, he asked me to make him a "black and yellow duck" costume, and I was happy to oblige.

But he was a big boy at five, and I felt a little wistful about his request. It was only a Halloween outfit, just a bit of red polyester and plastic. No big deal. But the costume would have no furry little ears to pull. No little tail, no whiskers. Not even a ducky beak to tweak.

Later in the evening as I was working in my office, he played his favorite game of "sneak." I heard him creeping along the floor and knew I would soon see his soft blond head poke up beside me as I sat at the computer. But instead, a cold red helmet popped up, followed by a muffled "*Boo!*" from behind a mask.

"Who is this?" I asked in feigned surprise.

"It's me!" the mask shouted.

"Who?" I asked again.

"Bwyce!" the mask answered.

"How do I know it's my boy Bryce?"

"Aw, Mom, see...." he answered, removing the mask and helmet. "It's me, Bwyce!"

I pulled him onto my lap. "How can you be my boy Bryce? You're getting so big!"

"Yup." He nodded solemnly. "That's the way it goes." I smiled at his words, as he parroted one of my oft-used expressions.

I ruffled his silky hair, squeezed him tight, and smothered his smooth cheeks with kisses. Maybe he's becoming a cool "big guy," but he'll always be my baby. That's the way it goes.

THERE IS A TIME FOR EVERYTHING, AND A SEASON FOR EVERY ACTIVITY UNDER HEAVEN ... A TIME TO EMBRACE AND A TIME TO REFRAIN.

ECCLESIASTES 3: 1, 5

God, help me know when to hold on and when to let go.

CHAPTER 15

Badges of Honor

As we grow old, the beauty steals inward.
—Ralph Waldo Emerson

The other day I received in the mail a "personal" letter from a well-known female celebrity. "Dear Cheryl," it began, "do you know what the biggest problem is for women after age thirty?"

Hmm. I began to wonder—marriage and parenting concerns? Career issues? Spiritual struggles? Nope. According to this movie-star friend, it's gravity. Gravity! Whereas I'm not fond of its ravages, I hardly consider it my biggest problem.

Nevertheless, gravity is beginning to take its toll on my "over thirty" body. One day, while I was standing half-dressed at the bathroom mirror, getting ready to go out, Sarah Jean watched intently.

"Mommy, why is the skin on your tummy all wrinkly like that?" she asked.

The stretch

marks of

pregnancy

are badges

of honor.

"Well, honey, my tummy had to stretch a lot when I was carrying you and your brothers before you were born, so the skin never went all the way back."

She pondered that explanation for a moment. "Kinda like a balloon that's lost its air, huh?"

What a painfully accurate description. "Uh—yes, dear, kind of like that."

"But, Mommy," she continued, "why are your knees all wrinkly?"

I looked down. By golly, they *were* getting wrinkly! Hmm. Now I was starting to get a bit discouraged.

"Well, honey, that's just what happens to your skin when you get a little older," I replied.

She looked me up and down for a few moments, blue eyes widening. "Will your *whole body* get like that?"

"Well, I suppose much of it will, eventually."

"Hmm," she said. "I guess your skin just gets tired and gives up, huh?"

HE HAS MADE EVERYTHING BEAUTIFUL IN ITS TIME.

ECCLESIASTES 3:11

Lord, thank you for enabling me to grow. May I see the stretch marks of pregnancy as badges of honor! Help me to see the beauty you see in all that you have made, including myself—and to celebrate the beauty and wisdom that comes with time.

CHAPTER 16

Green, Green Grass of Home

I am beginning to learn that it is the sweet, simple things of life which are the real ones after all.
—Laura Ingalls Wilder

I can't believe how dry this summer has been! My
lawn is so brown. I miss green grass." My friend
Janet sighed. Wisconsin was experiencing a record-
breaking drought.

"Come over to my house and you'll find green
grass—and pink and yellow grass too," I said.

My friend looked puzzled.

"Easter grass," I explained. "'Tis the season!"

Never mind that the Easter baskets were packed
away more than four months ago. The pesky plastic grass
still clings in the most unexpected places—under the
piano, in the toy box, sticking to bare feet. I find it in the

Cleaning the house while the kids are still growing is like shoveling the walk while it's still snowing.

clothes dryer lint trap and under the couch cushions. Yesterday I plucked a pink strand clinging to the back of my skirt as I headed off to church.

Just when I think I've cleaned up the last of the silver Christmas-tree icicles, Easter grass comes along to clog my vacuum cleaner.

But I'm not complaining. I recall being awakened too early on Easter mornings by noisy, pajama-clad children bouncing on my bed; dressing my sons in tiny bow ties and pinstriped vests and my daughter in a bonnet, shiny Mary Janes, and proper little white gloves. I feel a bit wistful remembering those bygone days. We no longer have bonnets, bow ties, and shiny Easter shoes. But we do still have the Easter baskets.

And grass.

So I thank God for pink plastic Easter grass. Even in August.

GIVE THANKS IN ALL CIRCUMSTANCES.
1 THESSALONIANS 5:18

For Easter grass that tangles my vacuum cleaner, for little sneakers that clutter the foyer, for smudges on the car windows, and tiny plastic toys that lurk under the coffee table, I give thanks, O Lord.

CHAPTER 17

Crayons in the Dryer

A good laugh is sunshine in a house.
—William Makepeace Thackeray

My daughter has always been enamored with miniature toys: tiny tea sets, itsy-bitsy dolls that live in heart-shaped lockets, pocket-size notebooks with teeny pens, and her little "Hello Kitty" crayon set, stored in a plastic pouch.

Those six little crayons, although miniature, did super-sized damage to a load of clothes in the dryer. I gasped in dismay as I sorted through the color-smeared laundry, planning just how I would scold my daughter as soon as she got home. Fortunately, most of that load was just towels, but I still didn't like them smeared with crayon! The green crayon did the most damage, as it had adhered to the collar of my husband's favorite golf shirt, a striped shirt he had had since bachelor-hood. As I peeled off the green glob, it became clear that the shirt was ruined.

Truth be told, I never liked that shirt anyway!

Since the only thing seriously marred was a shirt I was happy to discard, my daughter didn't receive the reprimand I had been planning. In fact, throwing out that shirt even seemed to improve my mood considerably!

Our children are watching to see how we react to life's mishaps.

Do you have a "something got left in a pocket and ruined the clothes in the dryer" story? Gum, lip gloss, perhaps a ballpoint pen? Almost every mother can recall such an incident. As the old adage, "No use crying over spilled milk," reminds us, there really is no use getting upset about it. How we react to such incidents can be very important, though, since our children learn from us how to deal with life's big and little annoyances.

Of course, we need to teach our children to learn from their mistakes and to prevent them in the first place. But more importantly, we can teach them resilience and perspective. We can show them how to clean up the mess, learn from the mistake, put the situation in perspective, and move on. And also to forgive. How we need to forgive! As our loving God forgives us, again and again and again.

CLOTHE YOURSELVES WITH COMPASSION, KINDNESS, HUMILITY, GENTLENESS AND PATIENCE. BEAR WITH EACH OTHER AND FORGIVE … ONE ANOTHER. FORGIVE AS THE LORD FORGAVE YOU.
COLOSSIANS 3:12–13.

Dear Lord, forgive me when I let little things upset me. Help me model to my children a kind and gentle spirit.

CHAPTER 18

This Mess Is a Place!

Cleaning and scrubbing can wait 'til tomorrow,
For babies grow up, we've learned to our sorrow,
So quiet down, cobwebs, dust, go to sleep
I'm rocking my baby and babies don't keep.

—Source unknown

W hile visiting my out-of-state brother and sister-in-law's home, Blake ran to one end of the room and exclaimed, "Look, everybody! A corner!"

This was a big deal to my young son, because he'd never seen an empty corner in our house. To say that our small home was overcrowded at the time would be an understatement. We had so many piles of stuff—piles of clothes, piles of toys, piles of books, pictures, dishes, papers—stuff! Since then we've built an addition onto our house, but I still have to be diligent about clutter.

When I can't stand the clutter anymore, I make the whole family go on a cleaning binge. This is usually motivated by the pending visit of a friend or relative whom we haven't seen in a while. We call this whirlwind of desperate housecleaning a "tornado." The trouble is, my husband and I sometimes have different ideas about what tidying entails. During one particularly intense and urgent tornado (a high school friend called to say she was in town and would be stopping by within five minutes), I caught Dave shoving magazines under the couch. When I called him on it, he argued, "Don't think of it as shoving magazines under the couch. Think of it as maximizing our home's storage capacity."

Hmm. Well, there was no time to argue with his logic.

I can't complain about my husband, though. In many ways, he's much tidier than I am. Now, lest you think I'm a slob, please understand that I'm a very clean person. I even enjoy cleaning. It's the *straightening up* that I find so tedious, trying to decide where to keep important things so I don't forget where I put them. I don't need a housecleaner; I need a house straightener—someone to decide where to put stuff. The problem is, I'd need this person to be around to help me find these things when I need them, since I often forget where I put them if they're stored out of sight.

I've finally cut myself some slack when it comes to tidiness. "Organized" is a relative term, I've learned. I recently read an encouraging article in a women's magazine that included a little self-test titled "Are You Organized?" To my delight, I learned I *am* organized—depending on how you define "organized." I scored high on this test, which asked the questions that matter, like "Do you get your kids to school on time?"; "Can you find important papers?"; and "If you volunteer for something, do you follow through?" I do all these things well, in spite of some household clutter.

I learned I'm a visual person who needs to see things to remember them. Thus, my kitchen bulletin board is covered with notices of things I need to do. Tidy people would put all these papers in a folder and remember to look at them. For me, it's "out of sight, out of mind."

The article noted that some people must have tidiness and predictability in order to function. Those of us who can function amid a certain amount of chaos are often more adaptable and adept at multitasking.

Don't get me wrong—I'm not criticizing tidy people. I admire them greatly. Many tidy people I know get a lot done in a day—and look great doing it. But it's nice to know that my system, too, can be defined as "organized."

It's just a different kind of organized.

Life isn't always tidy. In fact, real life often gets downright messy and unpredictable. Whereas the article gave excellent advice to help tidy the home, it also gave folks like me permission to relax a bit: If your system of organization works for you, your home functions well, and you're getting things done for your family that need to get done, then don't worry if your house doesn't look like a photo out of *House Beautiful*.

Having kids means sacrificing some tidiness.

I wish I'd kept that article. I'd have it framed.

Having kids means sacrificing some tidiness. Although the clutter in my home has diminished as my children have grown older, I still find new types of clutter constantly being created. Our family room, for example, would be much tidier if we moved the two computers there to the kids' bedrooms. But it makes good sense to me that the computers be kept in the hub of our home where we can monitor their use. Same thing with the television. Putting a television and VCR in the kids' bedrooms would keep the kids and their clutter out of the way. But I want the kids "in my way." In a few short years, they'll be gone. I'll take the clutter now.

When my children were younger, our refrigerator was always covered with their artwork, and we discovered that the front door also holds magnets, so it, too, was plastered with drawings. I didn't have the heart to require that "Lego masterpieces" be dismantled the same day they were created, so they frequently adorned the mantel and window ledges. The puzzles that took such time and concentration for little ones to piece together were left on the coffee table for several days to be admired by all who visited.

I ran into my friend Joanne one day at the shopping mall. At the time, we both had preschoolers. "I don't know what's wrong with me," I moaned. "Other mothers I know manage to keep their houses clean."

"Cheryl, you're just hanging around with the wrong people," Joanne quipped. "God gave you triplets because you can handle the chaos without going bonkers," she said. "A neat freak would be screaming for tranquilizers by now! Twenty years from now your children will remember the stories you told and the games you played, not whether you had a 'perfect' house."

I like Joanne. I'm glad she's my friend.

Excuse this house.

Some houses try to hide the fact that children
shelter there.

Ours boasts of it quite openly, the signs are
    everywhere!
For smears are on the windows, little smudges
    on the doors;
I should apologize, I guess, for the toys strewn
    on the floor.
But I sat down with the children today, and we
    played and laughed and read.
And if the doorbell doesn't shine, their eyes will
    shine instead;
For when I have to choose between one job or
    the other,
Though I need to cook and clean, first I'll be a
    mother.

—Author unknown

SHE WATCHES OVER THE AFFAIRS OF HER HOUSEHOLD AND DOES
NOT EAT THE BREAD OF IDLENESS.
PROVERBS 31:27

*God, help me organize my home in the way
that works best for my family. May it be a
place of harmony and peace.*

CHAPTER 19

Nice Words

Silent gratitude isn't very much use to anyone.
—G. B. Stern

My kids were playing nicely together, so I took advantage of the moment to rest for a few minutes. I grabbed a pillow and lay down in the hallway at the top of the stairs. From this spot I could spy on the children playing in the family room below without being noticed or, hopefully, interrupted.

After about five minutes, Bryce said to the others in his sweet lisp, "Come on, Sarah Jean; come on, Blake. Let's clean up the toys for Mommy." He then began to toss toys into the toy chest.

His siblings weren't helping. "Come on!" he urged. "Then Mommy will say, 'Oh what a nice surpwise!'"

Bryce tossed more toys into the chest before stopping

When we tell others we're grateful for their efforts, it inspires them to continue to do good works.

to say, "Okay, but if you don't help, you won't get any of Mommy's nice words!"

Oh—my heart completely melted! "Mommy's nice words!" I realized just how important our words of appreciation are. When we tell others we're grateful for their efforts, it inspires them to continue to do good works. It's so simple and yet so important to say thank you!

PLEASANT WORDS ARE A HONEYCOMB, SWEET TO THE
SOUL AND HEALING TO THE BONES.
PROVERBS 16:24

*God, guard my tongue —
Help me to choose uplifting words
That positively affect those around me
Like apples of gold.*

CHAPTER 20

Now We Can Play

Never does the human soul appear so strong
and noble as when it forgoes revenge and dares
to forgive an injury.

—E. H. Chapin

I was upstairs, keeping one ear on my five-year-olds playing in the family room. The sounds of noisy, rambunctious play were suddenly punctuated by a loud slap.

"I'm sorry!" Blake said.

There was no response from the injured brother.

"I'm sorry!" Blake repeated with urgency in his voice. A wise move on his part, considering his brother is bigger than he. Blake was genuinely remorseful, if not a little worried.

"I said I'm sorry," he persisted. "Now you have to say, 'I forgive you!'"

When we hurt someone, we need to apologize. And when forgiveness is granted, we can then move on.

"No!" Bryce retorted.

"But I said I'm sorry! Now you have to say, 'I forgive you!'"

"No, I won't say that!"

"Well, if you don't say, 'I forgive you,' then I'll ... I'll ... I'll take my 'I'm sorry' back!" Blake threatened.

There was a long pause as Bryce considered this threat. Finally, softly, reluctantly, he said, "I forgive you."

"Okay," Blake said matter-of-factly. "Now we can play."

Peace was restored.

I was amazed. I immediately ran for my notebook to write down the interchange. Someday, when I wonder if anything I have ever tried to teach them has stuck, I can remember that, at least this time, they got it right: When we hurt someone, we need to apologize. And when forgiveness is granted, we can move on. Then we can play.

BEAR WITH EACH OTHER AND FORGIVE WHATEVER GRIEVANCES
YOU MAY HAVE AGAINST ONE ANOTHER. FORGIVE AS THE LORD
FORGAVE YOU. AND OVER ALL THESE VIRTUES PUT ON LOVE,
WHICH BINDS THEM ALL TOGETHER IN PERFECT UNITY.

COLOSSIANS 3:13–14

*Loving God, you taught us to forgive as you
forgive us. May my children see in me the
ability to forgive and move on.*

CHAPTER 21

Rub a Dub Dub

The soul is healed by being with children.
—Fyodor Dostoevsky

We ought, every day at least, to hear a little
song, read a good poem,
and, if possible, speak a few reasonable words.
—Johann Wolfgang von Goethe

Read just about any article on how to beat stress, and you will likely be advised to soak away your stress in a bubble bath. Ah, what could be better? A sudsy, scented, sumptuous, soothing soak in the tub. Just the remedy for a stressed-out mom. Right?

"I'm going to take a bath," I announced to my family after dinner. "And I do not want to be disturbed for a full forty-five minutes. I'm not unlocking the door

CRAYONS IN THE DRYER

until eight thirty. Dave, you're in charge. Kids, if you have a question, ask Dad."

"A bath?" asked my daughter. "You never take a bath!"

"Well, I'm taking one now," I said as I ascended the stairs. "And I want peace and quiet."

Now, lest you get the wrong impression, I *do* bathe. But a long soak in the tub is a rarity. On a good day, I shower *and* condition my hair. On a really good day, I condition my hair for the full three minutes recommended by the bottle's instructions.

The upstairs bathroom, because it has the tub, became the kids' bathroom years ago. My pretty shell-shaped soap dish was long ago replaced by a mesh bin filled with tub toys. The kids claim they don't play with them anymore, but protested loudly when I suggested the toys be included in last spring's garage sale. But this evening, for one hour, it was to be *my* bathroom again.

I gathered the necessary accoutrements. Loofah. *Reader's Digest*. Bath pillow. Fluffy towel. I dusted off the pretty bottle of lavender bath salts one of the girls in my Scout troop had given me last Christmas. The fancy bottle hadn't even been opened because I never found the time for a bath that would last long enough to justify using the contents. But this evening I intended to soak until my toes were wrinkly.

I stepped into the sudsy water and slid down to my ears. Ahhhh.

Then came the knock on the door.

"I need my watch," Sarah Jean said through the door. "It's on the vanity."

"Why?"

"I need to time myself on how fast I can do my multiplication tables. I have a timed test tomorrow."

"Sweetheart, use the kitchen clock."

"Oh, okay."

Two minutes passed.

"Mom, I need you," Sarah Jean said.

"Are you done with your multiplication already?"

"It's only a two-minute test. You need to quiz me on my spelling."

"Ask Daddy to do it."

"He's helping Blake with his math."

"All right." I sighed.

The door handle wiggled.

"It's locked."

My pretty shell-shaped soap dish was long ago replaced by a mesh bin filled with tub toys.

"I know. I told you I'm not unlocking the door for forty-five minutes. Just slide the word list under the door." I quizzed her on the words twice, slid the list under the door, and settled back into the water.

"Mom, I hafta brush my teeth." It was Sarah Jean. Again.

"No, you don't. Bedtime isn't for half an hour."

"Daddy said to get ready for bed."

"Just get your pajamas on for now."

Silence. But I sensed her presence.

"Sarah Jean, are you still out there?"

"Yes."

"Why?"

"My pajamas are hanging on the back of the bathroom door."

"Go get some clean ones from your dresser."

Drowning out the sound of her fading footsteps were more feet stampeding up the stairs.

"Mom! Mom!"

"Is it an emergency?"

"Kind of!"

"Are you bleeding?"

"No ..."

"Then go away."

"Mo-o-o-m! Bryce said he'd trade me his Digometron card for four of my Blastotroid cards, but he took it back!" Blake hollered through the door.

"Mom, he took my *holographic* Digometron!" Bryce

yelled back. "I thought he meant my *plain* Digometron!"

"He's a cheater!"

"BOYS!" I interrupted. "Put all the cards on the kitchen table. We'll deal with it later. I want you to get your pajamas on now."

"But, Mom, it's not fair! Bryce said he would trade me—"

"Go! NOW!"

"Cheryl," my husband said apologetically, "sorry about the boys coming up here, but I was on the phone. Sarah Jean needs me to write a check for her lunch tickets. How much are they?"

"I think they're ten for seventeen fifty. Look in the PTA booklet in the middle desk drawer. It's a yellow booklet."

"Mom!" Sarah Jean called through the door. "Daddy can't find the PTA booklet."

"Why can't you take cold lunch tomorrow?"

"Cassie and Rhea are taking hot lunch tomorrow."

"Sarah Jean, don't bother your mother," my husband bellowed from the kitchen. I sighed, crawling out of the tub.

Now you know why I rarely take a bath. It's too stressful.

Love is patient.

1 Corinthians 13:4

111

Loving Creator,
You are so patient with me!
With each new moment
You give me another chance
To take a deep breath,
To gain perspective,
To readjust my attitude.
Remind me that the time with my children
Is a precious blessing every day.

CHAPTER 22

Sharing Ideas

Children are likely to live up to what you
believe of them.

—Lady Bird Johnson

once read that firstborn children can tend to be a little neurotic because their parents make all their
mistakes on them. I don't really believe that's true, but
if it is, then I have the potential for three equally neurotic children! So I listen, read, and learn all I can from
others. I incorporate what works for me into our lives
and ignore what doesn't apply.

My friends are a constant source of advice. Every
other month, we six gal pals meet at one of our homes
to get away, eat, commiserate, and laugh, laugh, laugh.
When it was my turn to host, I asked my friends to bring
their thoughts on parenting. They know I always have a

Get to know your child.

He changes quickly; he may be a different child today than he was yesterday.

book in the works and freely share their insight.

"Why do I get the feeling you are going to take notes tonight?" Gina asked, as we settled around the patio table.

"Okay," I confessed, pulling out my notepad. "I'm hoping to brainstorm a list of child rearing dos and don'ts for a chapter on mother wisdom. Since you're all so very wise, who better to ask?"

"Flattery will get you everywhere," Gina said, laughing and munching on a tortilla chip. "I think it's easier to start with what *not* to do." The others agreed, and here's what we came up with:

DON'TS
- Don't compare your child to his/her siblings.
- Don't give in to a child's whining. Instead try to find an alternative that makes you both happy.

- Don't say anything in front of your kids that you don't want repeated.
- Don't allow food in their rooms, except maybe "for special," like a sleepover.
- Don't allow television in the kids' rooms.
- Don't start the car until seatbelts are buckled.
- Don't feel guilty for saying no when it's the right thing to say.
- Don't use "Because I said so!" as a frequent response to "Why?"
- Don't try to mold your children into something they're not.
- Don't expect them to know more than their years allow them. They're kids.

Dos

- Do try to find a "yes" for every "no."
- Do listen to your kids. Even when they whine, ask them to tell you in an acceptable voice what's bothering them. Then listen.
- Do pray together before meals.
- Do have a special bag of toys that little ones only get to play with away from home.
- Do let them get dirty.
- Do require that they do chores. Kids need to feel needed—and you need their help.
- Do hug them even if they don't hug back.
- Do help them discover things they are good at,

and nurture those talents.

- Do say "I'm sorry" when you're wrong. Kids need to hear it.
- Do let them get bored. They'll get over it. Send them out to play.
- Do research movies, video games, and TV shows before granting permission to watch. (For movies, helpful sites are www.kids-in-mind.com and www.screenit.com. You also can trust movie reviews by renowned film critic Michael Medved at www.michaelmedved.com. For TV reviews, go to www.parentstv.org and www.pluggedinonline.com.)
- Do take "Mama time-outs." Leave the room when you're losing your cool.
- Do pick your battles. Ask yourself, *Will this matter five days—or five years—from now?*
- Do get to know your child's teachers.
- Do get to know your child's friends.
- Do get to know your child's friends' parents.
- Do make your kids write thank-you notes.
- Do keep a growth chart on a doorway or wall. It's a frequent reminder of how precious these child-rearing years are.
- Do say "I love you" often.

SHARING IDEAS

BY WISDOM A HOUSE IS BUILT, AND THROUGH UNDERSTANDING
IT IS ESTABLISHED; THROUGH KNOWLEDGE ITS ROOMS ARE
FILLED WITH RARE AND BEAUTIFUL TREASURES.
PROVERBS 24:3–4

*Lord, please put wise people in my life
from whom I can learn.*

CHAPTER 23

That's Not the Way Mommy Does It!

After God created the world, He made man and
   woman.
Then, to keep the whole thing from collapsing,
He invented humor.

—Guillermo Mordillo

Don't load the glasses on the bottom of the dishwasher," I'd hear myself saying to my husband.
Or, "You forgot the fabric softener."

Foolish me. That's a surefire way of discouraging
future help. I'm learning to bite my tongue and appreciate help in whatever form it's offered. Different isn't
always wrong; it's just different.

One night I was exceptionally tired. My level of
fatigue was surpassed, however, by the energy level of
my three toddlers, who shared a room at the time. This

particular night they were exceptionally rambunctious. Getting them tucked in was like corralling grasshoppers. I tried to cut the bedtime ritual short so I could get to bed myself.

"Mommy! You didn't tell us a story!" Every night, until they were six or so, I'd tell my kids a made-up-on-the-spot story after prayers. It might be a story about one of their stuffed animals, like Bunny Bing's Busy Day. Or Leah Ladybug Looks for a Lily. Although the stories weren't masterfully crafted, my kids always delighted in them.

But that night I was beyond tired. I was to-the-bone-can-hardly-walk exhausted. Yet how could I deny my cherubs their story?

"Well, I didn't tell you a story because tonight, for special, Daddy is going to tell the story," I announced.

They cheered, and I dragged myself downstairs to the kitchen, where my husband was working at his desk. "Honey, tonight you need to tell the kids a story."

Dave rose and headed for the kids' bookshelf in the family room.

"No, they want you to make up a story." Dave looked at me dubiously. "Go on," I urged. "You can do it."

Dave groaned. "Why can't I just read a book?"

"Because you're creating a precious memory." I yawned. "Go on. Just make up something."

So up he went. I plunked down at the breakfast bar and turned on the baby monitor. I wanted to hear this.

"Okay, guys," I heard over the scratchy monitor. "I get to tell the story tonight!" Three high-pitched voices cheered.

"So ..." Dave clapped his hands. "Here's the deal ..."

"No, Daddy," Sarah Jean interrupted. "That's not the way Mommy does it. You hafta say, 'Once upon a time ...'"

"Well, that's a fine story-starter for Mommy, but *my* stories start with, 'So, here's the deal.'"

Getting the kids tucked in was like corralling grasshoppers.

I couldn't wait to hear the rest of Daddy's story.

"So, here's the deal," Dave repeated, again clapping his hands. "Ahem.... Come and listen to a story about a man named Jed; a poor mountaineer, barely kept his family fed. And then one day he was shootin' at some food, and up from the ground came a-bubblin' crude! Oil that is! Black gold—Texas tea!"

I laughed, picturing the children lying wordlessly in their little toddler beds. Six blue eyes blinking wide in bewilderment, no doubt.

"Well, the first thing you know, ol' Jed's a millionaire," Dave droned on. "The kinfolk said, 'Jed, move away from there!' They said, 'Californey is the place ya oughta be.' So they loaded up the truck and they moved to Beverly. Hills that is. The end."

I heard him kiss each child: "Goodnight." Smooch. "Goodnight." Smooch. "Goodnight." Smooch. "I love you. Now go to sleep."

Dave returned to the kitchen with a satisfied grin.

I greeted him with an adoring hug.

"I enjoyed your story over the monitor. I think you should tell a story tomorrow night, too!"

"Okay." Dave shrugged. "I'm up for it. It's a story 'bout a man named Brady ..."

EACH ONE SHOULD USE WHATEVER GIFT HE HAS
RECEIVED TO SERVE OTHERS, FAITHFULLY ADMINISTERING
GOD'S GRACE IN ITS VARIOUS FORMS.
1 PETER 4:10

God, help me learn to delegate duties.
Help me appreciate the talents others
bring to our household.

CHAPTER 24

Yummy!

Happy is the person who can laugh at himself.
He will never cease to be amused.
— Harib Bourguiba

Each day of our lives we make deposits in the
memory banks of our children.
— Charles R. Swindoll, *The Strong Family*

My next-door neighbor Nancy was pleased that
her teenage daughter had taken an interest in
cooking. One evening Nancy came home to find that
Amy had fixed dinner. The family gathered around the
kitchen table and began enjoying the macaroni and
cheese she'd prepared.

"Uh, Amy," Nancy asked, midbite, "what did you
use to drain the macaroni?"

If we can't solve a problem, finding some humor in it is the next best thing; sometimes it's even better!

"The strainer, of course," Amy said.

"Where did you get it?"

"From the top rack of the dishwasher. I know the dishwasher hadn't run yet, but I figured you had just used the strainer to rinse fruit or vegetables or something, right?"

"Yechhhhh.... I used it to drain the fishbowl today!" Nancy choked.

This remark was immediately followed by the unison spitting of noodles and rinsing of mouths.

They ate sandwiches that night.

Years later that little mishap has become one of their favorite stories to retell when the family gets together. Because her parents created a loving environment, the entire family—including Amy—could see the humor in the situation, enjoy a good laugh, and still laugh about it today. A fun memory was created.

Not all families would have created a funny memory.

My friend "Joan" grew up in a household wrought with harsh ridicule. She once told me, "The first time I heard the expression, 'There's no use crying over spilled milk,' it confused me. When I was growing up, if the milk was spilled, someone had to be blamed, criticized, and certainly not forgiven. So when I heard that expression the first time as a teenager, it didn't even make sense to me. It was such a foreign concept."

Joan grew up feeling as though she was "walking on eggshells" all the time. As an adult, she discovered other people enjoyed life a whole lot more than she did.

"I noticed that other people could just move on when things go wrong, without getting mad. They could even laugh about them!" Thankfully, Joan now realizes that she doesn't have to continue this cycle of tension and blame and is determined to do better for her children.

"But it's really hard to break old habits," she confessed. "Growing up, I was never taught to find humor in everyday situations. I was taught to always place blame on myself or others."

It's been said that you grow up the day you have your first real laugh at yourself. If we can't solve a problem, finding some humor in it is the next best thing; sometimes it's even better. What a wonderful gift we can give our children—to create a loving, safe environment in which we can laugh with each other!

A CHEERFUL HEART IS GOOD MEDICINE,
BUT A CRUSHED SPIRIT DRIES UP THE BONES.

PROVERBS 17:22

Lord, bless my home with laughter. Help me teach my children to find the humor in everyday nuisances.

CHAPTER 25

Sharky

Feelings are everywhere—be gentle.

—J. Masai

Nothing valuable can be lost by taking time.

—Abraham Lincoln

How many fish should we put in the tank?" I asked. "Well, it depends on how big they are," the pet-store clerk explained. "Once your aquarium is established, you can add more, but for starters, I'd say two inches of fish per gallon. For your twenty-gallon tank, that'd be about nine or ten small fish. You'll want to choose from any of the aquariums along this wall." He waved his arm. "These are what we call 'community' fish. They should all get along with each other pretty well."

"Okay, kids," I announced. "You can each pick out three small fish." Sarah Jean and Bryce eagerly set to choosing their favorites.

"But I don't want a little fish. I want a Bala shark." Blake tugged at my jacket. "Mom, ask him about a shark."

"What if we got one of those Bala sharks?" I asked.

"Well, they can be a little aggressive, but if your tank's not crowded, a Bala would probably get along just fine."

"Okay, Blake, you can get a Bala," I said. "But since he's already over three inches long, it has to be your only fish. For now at least, until the tank gets established."

"That's okay. He's all I want anyway." Blake's eyes danced as the clerk netted his fish. He's a sensitive, rather quiet child, and it was sweet to see him so excited over his first pet.

The children could hardly wait to get home. Gathered around the aquarium, they named each fish. "I know what to call my Bala shark," Blake announced. "I'll call him Sharky! Actually, that'll be his last name. His first name is Friendly. Friendly Sharky. See how friendly he is with the little fish? He's sure a *good* shark."

Indeed, Sharky was a gentle shark. Our fears of him chasing or nipping at the smaller fish were quickly allayed. He never bothered them. In fact, he spent most of his time in one corner of the tank.

First thing every morning, the kids greeted their fish by name. After school they rushed to the aquarium to watch. They took turns each night feeding them. Several days later, after taking the children to school, I noticed Sharky wasn't looking so good. He was kind of listing to one side. I immediately called the pet store.

"I think our Bala is sick. Is there anything I can do?" I asked.

"Well, the tank might be too toxic for him. This can happen in new aquariums," the manager said. "You can try changing the water, but since he's already looking sick, it may be too late."

"It's worth a try. Thank you." I hung up and changed the aquarium water. When I returned to check on him an hour later, he had improved noticeably. There was hope!

By the time I'd picked the kids up from school, however, Sharky was lying motionless at the bottom of the tank. Sarah Jean and Bryce ran ahead to the aquarium, but I stopped Blake before he got there, hoping to break the news of Sharky's demise gently.

I knelt to look Blake in the eyes, holding his shoulders. "Blake, you know how Sharky didn't move around much? There's apparently a reason he wasn't very active—it's because—"

"Because he's dead!" Sarah Jean interrupted. I gave her a stern look. "Well, he is," she insisted. "He's really, really dead."

Blake ran to the aquarium. "Sharky! Oh no, poor Sharky! Why'd he die?" He blinked back tears.

"I know it's sad, honey, but these things happen." I put my arm around his shoulders. "Fish don't always last long."

"But he was such a good shark!"

"I know he was. We'll get another, okay? Now, let's get him out of there." Using the net, I scooped up the dead fish and dropped him in an empty jelly jar.

"What will we do with him now?" Blake asked.

"We could flush him," Sarah Jean suggested.

"In the *toilet?*" Blake squeaked, horrified.

"Well, you know it would be kind of a natural place for a fish—in the water, I mean," I offered weakly.

"Yeah, Blake, like a burial at sea!" Bryce exclaimed, trying to be helpful. He made a "whooshing" sound and dramatically pantomimed a flush.

"No, we're not gonna flush him! We need to have a funeral for him. We can bury him out in the woods," Blake said.

I agreed but told him we'd have to wait until after we returned from piano lessons. Until then, the jar holding Sharky would sit on top of the refrigerator, where it wouldn't get knocked over.

After piano lessons, we barely had time for supper before the kids' soccer practice. There was no time to bury Sharky.

The next day's schedule was filled with after-school

dentist appointments and an evening Cub Scout Pack meeting. Again, there was no time for a proper funeral, as Blake insisted the entire family be present for the ceremony. That night, after the kids were in bed, I took a peek at Sharky, telling my husband, "We've *got* to bury Sharky tomorrow. He's getting rather ... ripe."

"Put him in the freezer," Dave suggested.

"No, I'm not putting a dead fish in my freezer."

"What do you think fish sticks are?" Dave retorted. "Do you know what I think we should do with him?" he added.

"What?" I asked.

Dave cranked open the kitchen window and made a flinging motion. "Give him an *aerial burial*," he exclaimed with a flourish.

"I don't think that idea would *fly* with Blake," I quipped. "I'll put Sharky in the garage. Try to be home from work early tomorrow, and we'll bury him before supper."

The next evening, Blake held the jar containing Sharky high as he led the procession to the woods behind our house. Bryce followed with a shovel, and Sarah Jean shuffled along reluctantly, followed by Dave and me.

"This spot under the tree is perfect," Blake pronounced. "I'll always know where he is by this big tree."

We gathered around the tree as Blake dug a little hole and dumped Sharky in.

"Now I think we should all say something nice about Sharky," he said solemnly.

Bryce, who is demonstrative and enjoys being the center of attention, volunteered to go first. He cleared his throat, raised his index finger, and began his speech.

"Sharky was a fine, handsome, and well-behaved shark. His scales were so, so ... silvery. His tail was so ... flippy. He swam well and never complained...." Bryce continued to wax poetic until even Blake decided the oration had gone on long enough.

I know God cares for all his creatures.

"Okay, Bryce, my turn." Blake began his eulogy. "Sharky's full name was Friendly Sharky because he was friendly to all the little fish in the tank. He was my one and only shark, and I will miss him."

"Very nice, Blake," I said.

"Okay, Sissy, your turn," Blake said.

Sarah Jean rolled her eyes. "Sharky was ... a nice fish."

"And ..." Blake prompted.

She sighed. "He was a very nice fish."

"Okay," Blake said, satisfied. "Dad, your turn."

Dave stroked his mustache to hide his smile. Coughing several times so he wouldn't laugh, he offered some appropriate remarks about Sharky. Blake nodded in approval. "Mom, will you pray?"

"Um ... certainly." Unsure just what to pray over a fish, I assumed my most sincere, ministerial voice. "Lord, we thank you for the time we had together with Sharky. He brought joy to our family. May we always have fond memories of Sharky. Bless Blake, especially, as he mourns the loss of his dear fish."

"*Shark*, Mom," Blake whispered.

"As he mourns the loss of his dear shark. Amen."

Blake put a shovelful of dirt over his fish ... er ... shark, marking the spot with a stone.

We all looked at him for our cue, unsure what was expected of us next.

Blake ceremoniously folded his hands, bowed his head, closed his eyes, and declared solemnly, "And so it shall be."

At that Dave broke loose into a "coughing" fit.

"Didja swallow a bug, Dad?" Bryce asked, slapping him on the back.

"Yes, he must have," I said. "You kids run ahead and get him a drink of water. Quickly!"

I began pounding Dave on the back. "Don't you dare let them see you laugh," I hissed.

"Okay, I'm fine now. I think." He removed his glasses to wipe the tears. Placing his glasses back on his face, he peered at me over the rims and in a deep voice said, "And so it shall be!"

That night, as I tucked him into bed, Blake asked, "Do you think Sharky's in heaven?"

I chose my words carefully. "Well, I don't know if fish go to heaven or not. But I know God cares for all his creatures, and we'll always have our happy memories of Sharky."

"Yeah." Blake sighed contentedly. "And Mom?"

"Yes?" I answered.

"It sure was a great funeral, wasn't it?"

"Yes, it sure was," I said, kissing him on the forehead. Certainly a memory had been made that our family would recall for years to come.

A TIME TO WEEP AND A TIME TO LAUGH,
A TIME TO MOURN AND A TIME TO DANCE.
ECCLESIASTES 3:4

Loving Father, help me to remember to be compassionate and gentle with others' feelings and to take time for the things that matter most ... not just the things that matter most to me, but to those I love.

CHAPTER 26

Christmas of My Dreams

Somehow, not only for Christmas, but all the year through
The joy you give to others is the joy that comes back to you.
—John Greenleaf Whittier

W e've *got* to get this house cleaned by Christmas!"
I declared to my husband.

Dave looked up from his desk, glanced at the family room, and asked wryly, "This Christmas?"

I scanned the cluttered room. Play-Doh animals were drying on the breakfast bar, ABC magnets were stuck not only to the refrigerator but to all the kitchen chair legs as well. A "zoo" of stuffed animals had occupied one corner of the family room for more than a week. A "castle" of large cardboard blocks threatened to topple over in another corner. Stacks of picture books were piled on the coffee table.

I sighed as I slumped down on the well-worn couch.

"At least we didn't have to put a fence around the tree this year," Dave offered. I smiled, remembering the various ways we tried to keep our past trees triplet proof, including suspending them from the ceiling.

Along with the gifts the Wise Men bring are three nickels and two candy canes.

"That's true," I agreed, surveying the towering Scotch pine. It was enormous, brushing the ceiling. The Christmas-tree-farm owner said this would be his last year selling trees, so all the trees were the same price, regardless of size. Dave and I got caught up in the children's enthusiasm and ended up cutting the biggest one we could find. The children had hung most of the ornaments on the bottom third of the tree, so the star on top looked mighty lonely.

Dave plugged in the tree lights and squeezed next to me on the couch, amid some animals that had escaped from the zoo. We gazed at the tree, its bottom-heavy branches sagging. That afternoon I had tried to help the children make ornaments by covering cardboard stars with aluminum foil. They decided, however, that it was quicker to ball up wads of foil and throw them into the branches. They had used up an entire roll of foil making a couple dozen of these unusual ornaments.

"I actually thought that this year I'd try out an idea I saw in a magazine," I said with a laugh. "I was going to weave gold ribbons throughout the branches, with sprigs of dried baby's breath."

"Uh … I don't think it's gonna happen this year," Dave said. "You know what your dad would say."

"I think this is the nicest tree we've ever had!" we both recited in unison. My dad said that every year about my parents' tree.

I sighed again and snuggled closer to my husband. It was the nicest tree we'd ever had—foil wads and all.

"The Christmas of My Dreams"

The Christmas cookies all are frosted,
    the gingerbread men have purple hair—
And because little hands can only reach so high,
    the top half of the tree is quite bare!
But the bottom half sparkles with tinsel
    and foil stars and paper chains,
And along with the gifts the Wise Men bring
    are three nickels and two candy canes.

Although it's true our money's tighter than ever,
    our love just keeps on growing, it seems—
And I couldn't ask for anything more,
    this is the Christmas of my dreams.

I used to have such great expectations
    about Christmas and just how it should be,
With the picture perfect table of goodies
    and lots of presents under the tree.
Although I still love the tinsel and glitter,
    the scent of pine, and songs in the air,
When all's said and done, what matters most
    is the Christmas Love that all of us share.
Although our Christmas may not be very fancy,
    like the ones you see in magazines,
I wouldn't trade it for anything,
    this is the Christmas of my dreams.

So let's each count our blessings,
    and thank our God above,
As we celebrate this season of
    the Greatest Gift of Love.
Our Christmas may not be very fancy,
    like the ones you see in magazines,
But I couldn't ask for anything more,
    this is the Christmas of my dreams.
                        ©1994 Cheryl Kirking/Mill Pond Music

THANKS BE TO GOD FOR HIS INDESCRIBABLE GIFT!
2 CORINTHIANS 9:15

There are so many distractions at Christmastime, Lord. Help me and my family focus our hearts on you. May we experience a joyful celebration of your precious gift of redeeming love, and may we share that love abundantly.

CHAPTER 27

Think of the Children First

We all have only one life to live on earth.
Through television, we have the choice of
encouraging others to demean this life or to
cherish it in creative, imaginative ways.

—Fred Rogers

*O*ne of the greatest dignities of humankind is that
each successive generation is invested in the wel-
fare of each new generation," said Fred Rogers, beloved
creator of the children's show *Mr. Rogers' Neighborhood.*
"Those of us in broadcasting have a special calling to
give whatever we feel is the most nourishing that we
can for our audience. We are servants of those who
watch and listen."

As parents, we, too, have "a special calling to give
whatever we feel is the most nourishing that we can" for
our kids. Television and other electronic media can be a

tool to "cherish life," as Mr. Rogers said. But it won't happen without effort on our part. It takes a significant investment of time to find quality programming for our kids to watch. Sometimes it feels like trying to keep the ocean back with a teaspoon. But try, we must. My friend "Debra" (I'll keep her real name private) assured me I'm not alone, as she described for me the exchange that recently took place in her home.

We need each other's help to set a higher standard for our children's entertainment.

"Paige said her mom thinks you're too strict," Debra's thirteen-year-old daughter, Molly, said.

Irritated, Debra willed herself not to sound defensive. "Oh? How did that come up in conversation?"

"Paige said her mom thinks it's ridiculous that you have to check out every movie I see."

Debra had explained to her daughter in the past that not all PG-13 movies are suitable for thirteen-year-olds. In fact, many were in poor taste, regardless of one's age.

"So far, Molly has respected the guidelines we've

set for her," Debra said. "But it's getting harder, as it seems like watching videos is the main thing kids want to do when they get together." Indeed, it's up to us to help our kids find good options for fun.

We need each other's help to set a higher standard for our kids' entertainment. Mr. Rogers said, "Please think of the children first. If you ever have anything to do with their entertainment, their food, their toys, their custody, their day or night care, their health care, their education—listen to the children, learn about them, learn from them. Think of the children first."

WHATEVER IS TRUE, WHATEVER IS NOBLE, WHATEVER IS RIGHT,
WHATEVER IS PURE, WHATEVER IS LOVELY, WHATEVER
IS ADMIRABLE—IF ANYTHING IS EXCELLENT OR
PRAISEWORTHY—THINK ABOUT SUCH THINGS....
AND THE GOD OF PEACE WILL BE WITH YOU.
PHILIPPIANS 4:8–9

God, I need your help! Give me the strength to say no to harmful media, and help us find positive entertainment for our children. May our home be a sanctuary of your goodness and love.

CHAPTER 28

This Little Light of Mine!

Make the most of yourself, for that is all there is of you.

—Ralph Waldo Emerson

Now it's time to go to sleep," I said as I tried to back out of the door to my three-year-olds' room. I'd already told three stories; listened to three very long prayers; kissed three teddy bears, a giraffe, a bunny, and a penguin; fetched three glasses of water; and sent the children on three trips to the bathroom.

"But, Mommy," Bryce pleaded, "I've gotta tell you something important!"

"Go to sleep," I replied firmly.

"But, Mommy, it's really important. You gotta come here!"

"What is it, Bryce?"

"You hafta come here!" he persisted.

"What is it?" I repeated, kneeling beside his toddler bed. Taking my face in his soft, dimpled hands, he looked me in the eyes and whispered, "Mommy, don't ever hide your light under a biscuit!"

I assured him that I would not.

God has called us to be the light of the world.

"He means basket," Sarah Jean explained from across the room. "Our Sunday school teacher said a bushel is a kind of basket."

"We sang about that," offered Blake from the third little bed, as he broke into an enthusiastic rendition of "This Little Light of Mine," complete with actions to the verse, "Hide it under a bushel, NO!"

"That's right, Mommy," Bryce repeated. "Don't you ever hide your light under a biscuit! Let it shine, let it shine, let it shine!"

After three more kisses, I finally made it back downstairs to enjoy a quiet moment over a cup of tea and muse over Bryce's bedtime remarks. I thought of times I'd failed to serve others because I wasn't paying attention to their needs. I recalled times that I'd held back because I felt insecure about my abilities.

And I prayed that God might help me and my children offer our "little lights" to others, never hiding them under bushels. Or, for that matter, biscuits!

HE SAID TO THEM, "DO YOU BRING IN A LAMP TO PUT IT UNDER A BOWL OR A BED? ... WITH THE MEASURE YOU USE, IT WILL BE MEASURED TO YOU—AND EVEN MORE."

MARK 4:21, 24

Loving Creator, you have called us to be the light of the world. May I be a light of love to my children. May their lives shine your goodness, that you may be glorified.

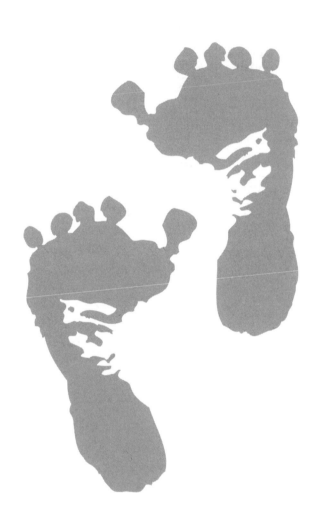

CHAPTER 29

Shine on the One I Love

If you can give your children a trust in God they will have one sure way of meeting all the uncertainties of existence.

—Eleanor Roosevelt

Leaning on the railing of the deck that overlooks our backyard, I breathed in the cool night air as I gazed at the near full moon shining above. The lullaby I had sung to my children so many times played in my head and became my prayer.

I see the moon; the moon sees me
Down through the leaves of the big oak tree.
Please let the light that shines on me
Shine on the one I love.

It had been five of the longest days of my life as a mother.

Nine-year-old Sarah Jean was gone on her first weeklong camping experience.

She was nervous about going, but excited. We arrived early so we could meet the camp director, who greeted her with a hearty handshake and a broad smile. "Julie's one of the very best counselors we've ever had. You're going to love her!"

I could see that Sarah Jean's confidence was bolstered, and she couldn't wait to meet her counselor.

As campers began to arrive and register, we hauled her gear to her assigned cabin. The other girls arrived in pairs: Two, four, six girls quickly filled the other bunk beds, leaving just one empty bunk for the counselor.

Sarah Jean was the only little girl who hadn't come to camp with a friend.

As I listened to the other mothers chat, I quickly realized they were all members of the same church. Sarah Jean figured that out too.

"Mom," she whispered, "everybody knows each other."

"That's okay, sweetie," I whispered back. "You'll get to know the other girls. Your counselor will make sure of it."

Just then the counselor arrived. Her name wasn't Julie; it was Hannah. "Julie had to go home suddenly,"

Hannah explained. "She's got the stomach flu. She hopes it's just a twenty-four-hour thing and that she'll be back tomorrow or the next day."

After discreetly informing Hannah that Sarah Jean was a first-time camper and, unlike the other girls, didn't know anyone else, I left with Hannah's promise to make sure my daughter wasn't lonely.

"Hannah seems real nice," I whispered again in my daughter's ear. "Don't you think?"

Sarah Jean nodded hesitantly as I gave her one last kiss and hug.

That was Sunday.

I felt uneasy all day Monday and Tuesday, but told myself I was just being overly concerned.

On Wednesday, the camp nurse called.

"Has Sarah Jean had problems with hives in the past?" the nurse asked. "I don't see any allergies listed on her health form."

"No, she doesn't have any allergies, and she's never had hives. Could it be nerves?"

"Well, that's certainly possible," the nurse said. "The heat may be a factor, as well. It's been in the nineties every day and just isn't cooling off at night. In fact, I've had the entire camp sleep in the lodge the last two nights. It's the only place that's air-conditioned. We've had quite a few sick kids this week. I'm not sure if it's the heat or the flu."

"Do you think I should come get her? If you think I

should, I'll drive right down," I offered, half hoping the nurse would say yes.

"No, I don't think that's necessary. But I'll keep an eye on her and let you know if she seems sick," she answered kindly.

I hung up the phone feeling like the worst mother in the world. My poor daughter was hot, lonely, and covered with hives!

On Thursday morning, I thought I'd just touch base with the camp director.

"Well, Mrs. Kirking, I'll check on Sarah Jean—I'm sure she's fine. I'll call you back," he said.

I wasn't so sure, but I didn't want to be one of "those" mothers—the worrying, overly cautious type.

Finally the camp director called me. "You know, Mrs. Kirking, I checked on Sarah Jean at lunchtime today, and other than a few hives, she's fine. She was a little tearful, though. She asked to call home, but we try to discourage that."

"I understand," I said. "I was a camp counselor myself. I know it's important for her to get over the homesickness, to see that she can do it, but still...."

"I will say it's been a challenging week, with the heat wave and the flu that's going around. Uh ... I should probably tell you I just realized that Sarah Jean is in the cabin that has had three different counselors this week, as they've been getting sick one by one. Julie's back today, though."

Three different counselors in five days! No wonder my daughter, who likes things to be predictable, was covered with hives.

"Would it be possible for me to speak with Julie? It would put my mind at ease."

"Absolutely! I'll have her call you at rest time this afternoon."

I fretted for the next couple of hours, waiting for the counselor's call. Was my concern justified? Was it mama instinct or needless worry that gnawed at my heart? It had to be a miserable week for Sarah Jean. My little sweetie was tearful. She wanted to call home. None of her string of flu-ridden counselors would know that she hadn't come with a friend. She had the hives. What kind of an awful mother was I, making my daughter suffer so? I was the one who had talked her into going to camp. I'd told her she'd have fun; she'd never trust me again!

Please let the light that shines on me shine on the one I love.

At two thirty, the phone finally rang.

"Hi, Mrs. Kirking, this is Sarah Jean's counselor, Julie." Her voice was warm and friendly. "I guess you

153

wanted to talk to me about Sarah Jean?"

"Yes, Julie. And thank you for calling. I hear you've had kind of a rough week too?"

"Yes, but I'm better now." Julie certainly sounded sweet.

"I don't know if anyone mentioned this to you, but I just wanted to let you know that this is Sarah Jean's first camping experience, and when we dropped her off I noticed all the other girls in the cabin knew each other. I mentioned this to the first counselor, Hannah, and she was going to make sure that Sarah Jean wasn't left out—but Hannah got sick the first day. So, I just wanted to touch base. I don't want to be an overly worried mom, but the nurse said Sarah Jean has hives and—"

"Oh, I'm so glad you told me! I just got here, and I assumed all the girls knew each other from their church," Julie said. "Sarah Jean seems to be well liked and doing fine, but I'll make extra sure that she's doing okay."

I hung up feeling somewhat relieved, certain that Julie would do her best to make the remaining two days good ones for Sarah Jean.

I again breathed in the cool night air, grateful the heat wave had finally broken. I was grateful, too, for Julie's call. I realized that in all my worrying, although I had prayed constantly the last few days, I hadn't allowed myself to feel God's peace and truly trust my daughter in his care. I needed to do that now and

remember she was being loved by and watched over by
the divine Creator who hung the moon in the sky.

CAST ALL YOUR ANXIETY ON HIM BECAUSE HE CARES FOR YOU.
1 PETER 5:7

*Dear Lord, please help me to teach my
children of your unfailing love; help them to
know that, even when we're far apart, you are
holding them in your loving arms. May they
always know your ever-present
comfort and peace.*

CHAPTER 30

An Older Mother Speaks

An ounce of mother is worth a pound of clergy.
—Spanish proverb

I hear my daughter shriek from the backyard, and I bolt out the door to investigate. Has someone fallen, broken an arm, or worse? No, just a noisy game of "Monster Chase." I breathe a sigh of relief.

The children come home from playing with friends with a new word in their vocabulary: gross. *I shudder at what they may learn next. Their little hearts are so tender!*

On the whole, I'm not a worrier. I'm really quite a calm, cool, collected mother—as long as my children are within my field of vision, and I control all they eat, breathe, see, and do.

Give your children God.

"When do you stop worrying about your kids?" I asked Debra and Sharon, my wise friends and the mothers of grown children.

They looked at each other with knowing smiles.

"You never stop worrying, but you worry less," said Debra.

"My mom says that you hold your children in your prayers when you can't hold them in your arms," Sharon added. "But I confess, I still worry. It gets better. It's a part of the mothering process."

I'm still very much in the middle of this process. The following poem has helped me along the way. I hope it will help you, too.

An Older Mother Speaks

They come to me with questions in their eyes,
These mothers of small daughters and sons;
They tell me of their longing to be wise
In rearing their own precious little ones.
And I who have lived longer, far, than they,
Who understand their seeking hearts so well,
Look backward through the long years that I may
Find something wise and beautiful to tell.

And always there is God; I speak of Him.
Without His help no mother's heart could bear
The anxious hours, the swift bright days abrim
With grave responsibility and care.
And if I had no other word to give,
After the winding roadways I have trod,
This would be my message: while you live,
O dear young mothers, give your children God.

—Grace Noll Crowell

MAY YOUR UNFAILING LOVE REST UPON US,
O LORD, EVEN AS WE PUT OUR HOPE IN YOU.
PSALM 33:22

*Lord, help me guide my children to
a faith in you.*

CHAPTER 31

If I Could Hold This Moment

Life affords no greater responsibility, no greater
privilege, than the raising of the next generation.
—C. Everett Koop, MD

L ittle one, so soft—close your sleepy eyes
Breath of an angel, gentle baby sighs
Go to sleep my love, I will sing a lullaby
When you wake or if you cry, I'll be here ...

If I could hold this moment and keep it for my own,
Surely this precious moment is the sweetest that I've
known.
The softness of your tiny hand, the warm scent of your
hair,
I delight in your babyhood, but I can't keep you there.
For other voices call, and you've so much more to grow,

So I'll learn to gather memories
 as I learn to let you go.

Little one, you've grown, strong
 and good and bold,
Off to find adventure, discover-
 ies untold.
Run and play, my love, here's a
 kiss to take along.
I'll watch from the window, I'll
 be here.

I'll learn

to gather

memories as

I learn to let

you go.

If I could hold this moment and
 keep it for my own,
Surely this precious moment is the sweetest that I've
 known!
To hear your laughter as you play, the sunlight in your
 hair,
I delight in your childhood, but I can't keep you there.
For other voices call, and you've so much more to grow,
So I'll learn to gather memories as I learn to let you go.

©1992 Cheryl Kirking/Mill Pond Music

IN HIM OUR HEARTS REJOICE, FOR WE TRUST IN HIS HOLY NAME .

PSALM 33:21

Time Well Spent

"I didn't get anything done today," I lamented to my husband after tucking the kids in. "I still have stuff on my to-do list from four days ago!"

I'm a list maker. I get a sense of accomplishment as I cross off each daily task. And I find if I don't make lists, I forget to do some of the most basic things, like pay a bill or buy milk and eggs.

Every book I've read on organizing encourages list making, and that's good advice. But most of the magical moments of mothering take place between the tasks we scratch off our to-do lists. These are things we don't put on our list but that bless our lives or the lives of those we love in ways we could never predict. Things such as:

- making a batch of salt dough for bored toddlers on a rainy day;

- listening to your teenager's account of her miserable day at school;
- making "people sandwiches" with the couch cushions;
- going outside to look for robins on an unseasonably warm March day;
- wrapping a child in a bath towel toasty from the dryer.

It's easy to get discouraged when we measure our accomplishments by how many items got crossed off the daily to-do list. Perhaps we'd be wise to keep a separate list of all the things we accomplished that weren't on the list. This new list is the one that would point us to everyday glimpses of grace and joy.

Time Well Spent

Are you a mother? Do you ever wonder
   if you accomplish much each day
When you see the floor that didn't get mopped,
   or the laundry still not put away?
If you sometimes feel discouraged,
   I've a few questions to ask of you;
Perhaps it's time to take a look
   at all the things you do.

Did you fold a paper airplane?
   Did you wash a sticky face?
Did you help your child pick up toys
   and put them in their place?

Did you pull a wagon, push a swing,
    or build a blanket tent?
If so, let me tell you that your day was quite well spent.

Did you turn the TV off and
    send the children out to play?
And then watch them from the window
    as you prayed about their day?
When they tracked mud on your kitchen floor,
    did you try hard not to scold?
Did you snuggle close as prayers were said
    and bed time stories told?

Did you wipe away a tear?
    Did you pat a little head?
Did you kiss a tender cheek as you tucked
    your child in bed?
Did you thank God for your blessings,
    for your children, heaven sent?
Then rest assured, dear mother,
    your time was quite well spent.

Did you make sure they brushed their teeth today?
    Did you comb tangles from her hair?
Did you tell them they should do what's right,
    though life's not always fair?
Did you quiz her on her spelling words, as you tried
    hard not to yawn?
Did you marvel at how tall he is,
    and wonder where the childhood has gone?

Did you buy another jug of milk?
    Was that broccoli you cooked?

Did you straighten your son's tie
    and say how handsome he looked?
Did you hold your tearful daughter
    when her teenage heart was broken?
Did you help her find some peace of mind,
    although few words were spoken?

Did you help him choose a college
    and get the applications sent?
Did you feel a little wistful at
    how quickly the years went?
Did you help her pack a suitcase
    and try hard not to cry?
Did you smile and smooth her hair
    as you hugged her goodbye?

Do you hold them in your prayers
    although your arms must let them go?
Do you tell them that you love them,
    so they will always know?
To make a home where love abides
    is a great accomplishment
And to serve God as a mother
    is to live a life well spent.

©2000 Cheryl Kirking

A MAN REAPS WHAT HE SOWS.... LET US NOT BECOME WEARY
IN DOING GOOD, FOR AT THE PROPER TIME WE WILL REAP
A HARVEST IF WE DO NOT GIVE UP.

GALATIANS 6: 7, 9

Readers' Guide

For Personal Reflection
or Group Discussion

Readers' Guide

Being a mother is a journey and an evolving process, full of ups and downs. You face many new decisions, emotions, opportunities for growth, responsibilities, and stresses. And how you respond to your changing and growing children makes a huge difference in their lives today and in who they will become tomorrow. No doubt that's one reason why you picked up this book.

Cheryl Kirking understands. She lives in a world of triplets and isn't afraid to tell it like it is.

As you answer the following questions, realize that you are not alone! Other mothers (including Cheryl) face the same issues you probably face: how to keep children's treasures from taking over a home; recognizing and encouraging a child's uniqueness; learning to trust God and receive his love; the importance of laughter; breaking cycles of shame and criticism; using words carefully; discovering joy; and many others.

As you ponder these questions, and possibly discuss

them with other mothers, answer them honestly. They are designed to guide you into personal reflection and aid you in growing stronger relationships with your family and with God. Truths hidden within simple questions may open up whole new perspectives concerning yourself, family members, other people, and God.

Feel free to adapt these questions to your particular situation. Perhaps you'll think about and/or discuss one or two in great depth, and spend less time on others. That's okay. Where you are right now will influence which questions especially connect with you. Although your experiences may be quite different from those of Cheryl or other mothers mentioned in this book, you may be surprised by the points of connection that appear.

Sometimes you may smile as you identify with the author's feelings or a particular event she experiences with her children. Perhaps tears may come as you recognize situations in which you could have handled things differently—within yourself, toward your children, toward God. No matter where you are—as a mother, as a single parent or wife—remember that God is who he says he is. He loves you and your children and longs to be in a living, dynamic relationship with you. He desires to share his power, comfort, and blessings with you and make you a blessing to others.

When it comes to parenting, no magic formulas work for everybody. But you can find unexpected, everyday blessings ... celebrate special moments ... and receive valuable truths that continue to stand the test of time.

CHAPTER ONE

1. What are *your* dreams and expectations of motherhood?

2. To which mother(s) are you tempted to compare yourself? Why?

3. Why is comparing yourself to other "perfect" mothers self-defeating?

4. As you read Colossians 3:2, what did you think about? How might remembering this verse make difficult times a little easier?

5. How do God's standards for being a good mother differ from other people's standards?

CHAPTER TWO

1. What kinds of very good things can usurp our time with our children if we are not careful?

2. Cheryl mentioned the time watching the fish eat as when she listens to her children. When are the best times for you to listen to your children? Why?

3. When do you find it hard to say *no* in order to keep your children a top priority?

4. How do you determine which things in your life should have the highest priority? If you have a hard time doing this, who might you turn to for help?

5. How might God fit into the picture when setting priorities is difficult?

CHAPTER THREE

1. When you read the word *quietude*, what came to mind? Why?

2. In a given week, how much time do you spend on "pause"? What do you do, or what could you do, to regain personal equilibrium when life seems out of control?

3. Why are so many mothers uncomfortable when they are not *doing* something "productive"?

4. Reread Psalm 46:10 and Matthew 11:28. Why do you think God reminds us to "be still"? To what extent do you believe God cares about how you feel? What does he promise to do if you come to him?

CHAPTER FOUR

1. When do you feel insecure in mothering, thinking you don't know nearly enough? Which situations tend to bring out your insecurities?

2. Which mother has taught you the most—about what to do or what not to do in various situations? Describe a time when you learned a key lesson that has helped you with your children.

3. What are the three most important lessons you've learned about motherhood so far?

4. Which things might you add to the author's humorous list of what she has learned through "real-life mothering"?

5. Describe an unexpected lesson you've learned lately that especially blessed you.

CHAPTER FIVE

1. What happens if we focus too much on what a child will become instead of focusing on who he or she is today?

2. Think about your children. What are you most thankful for?

3. Why do some people tend to focus on the challenges of motherhood rather than the joys? To what extent do you focus on the joys? On the difficulties? Why?

4. How can we show our children that we view them as blessings?

5. Where does joy come from? How is it different from happiness?

CHAPTER SIX

1. What reminds you to "hang in there" and work with a grateful, joyous heart?

2. The author told a story that linked children's training to their responses later in life. Describe a time when your parent(s) taught you a lesson that you never forgot.

3. Why did the author keep the broken pencil? How does this story relate to us today?

4. Would the people closest to you say that you have a positive attitude toward parenting? Why or why not?

5. Which emotional area(s) might you need to work on in order to become more godly and positive?

CHAPTER SEVEN

1. What do you think Henry Ward Beecher meant when he wrote, "A mother's heart is a child's schoolroom"?

2. Why is it important to remember that, in everything we do, we are modeling attitudes and actions for our children?

3. Do you believe kindness is "caught," not taught? Why or why not?

4. How did you feel as you read the poem, "By a Child"?

5. As you were growing up, who demonstrated positive actions that influenced you? If you are discussing these questions in a group, share a situation in which an adult's actions taught you an important principle.

6. Sometimes as children we learned lessons because other people hurt us. Why is it important, as adults, to work through that pain rather than burying it deep inside?

7. What hope is found in Proverbs 22:6?

8. Why is it important for us to ask for, and receive, God's powerful love every day? What happens if we try to love people in our own strength?

CHAPTER EIGHT

1. What is involved in *really* listening?

2. Would you say that you are a good listener? Why or why not? (Be honest!)

3. How can we discover whether we listen well?

4. When we listen intently to our children, what do we communicate? What do we encourage them to do?

5. What kinds of things hinder us from listening well?

6. How well did your parent(s) listen to you as you were growing up? How did that make you feel?

CHAPTER NINE

1. What's the difference in attitude between "molding" a child and "unfolding" a child? Explain your answer.

2. What can we do when a child's personality is completely different from ours and we can't figure out what to do? If you are in a group, discuss some ways in which mothers can learn about personality types and real-life examples.

3. Why don't "cookie-cutter" approaches to raising children work? What can happen when parents impose such approaches on their children? (If you feel comfortable doing so, share an example from your life.)

4. What does Jeremiah 1:4 reveal? Why is this truth important to understand?

5. When do you find it hard to view your children as a holy miracle from God? Where does God fit in when you are having a particularly stressful time parenting?

CHAPTER TEN

1. What are your favorite memories from your childhood? Why?

2. The author wrote down favorite incidents in order to "capture" them. Would this be a fun thing for you to do? Why or why not? If not, how might you capture family memories? (A photo album? A digital camera?)

3. How aware are you of "unexpected blessings" your children give you? What may be causing you to miss memories?

4. Do you think it's possible to create times when special moments can provide opportunities for special memories? Why or why not?

5. If recording a child's special moments or words seems like another burdensome "to-do" item to you, what might that indicate?

CHAPTER ELEVEN

1. As we watch our children grow, why is our faith in God and his promises so important?

2. When you feel as if you are stumbling, to whom can you turn?

3. What happens when we try to "hold our children's hands" too much? Too little?

4. Reread Psalm 37:23–24.
   • What's the difference between "stumbling" and "falling"?

- What delights the heart of God?

- According to the Bible, what can we do to encourage our children to cling tightly to God?

CHAPTER TWELVE

1. How do we find the balance between being firm and being overbearing? If you are discussing this in a group, share examples of when you disciplined wisely and unwisely.

2. What is involved in speaking "with wisdom," as Proverbs 31:26 instructs? What is "faithful instruction"?

3. Define "firm instruction balanced with love." What day-to-day challenges do we face as we try to provide this kind of instruction?

4. In her prayer, the author mentioned the "holy privilege" of being a mother. What do you think she meant by this?

5. If someone tape-recorded the instructions you give your children every day for a week, what kinds of things would you enjoy hearing later? What would you wish you'd never said?

CHAPTER THIRTEEN

1. How can we prepare for difficult questions?

2. Why is it important for us to discover the meaning behind our children's questions? How do we do that?

3. If we don't know the answer to a child's question, how might we respond?

4. When we brush over a child's question without really answering it, what are we communicating?

5. How important is it to answer children's questions honestly? Why?

6. What can each of us do to become more sensitive to the Holy Spirit's guidance?

CHAPTER FOURTEEN

1. How did you learn responsibility as a child?

2. What are the "wings of independence" we need to give our children? Why are they so important?

3. As you think about the time when your children will be independent, what do you feel? Why?

4. How long do you think it takes to teach a child to handle responsibilities effectively? To teach a child the attitudes and skills necessary to become independent?

5. Reread Ecclesiastes 3:1, 5. What do you think these verses mean? How do they apply to motherhood and raising children?

6. Why is it so important for us to take parenting one day at a time?

CHAPTER FIFTEEN

1. How do you feel about your physical condition? Why?

2. Given your unique situation, what can you do to keep yourself in shape physically—or get back into shape?

3. What does it mean to be *beautiful* in our culture? Contrast this with the inner beauty Ralph Waldo Emerson mentioned in the introductory quote.

4. Define some characteristics of inner beauty and think about how they are formed.

5. As our bodies age, is it realistic to think we can celebrate our inner beauty? Explain your answer.

CHAPTER SIXTEEN

1. Are you pretty good at treasuring sweet and simple things in life? Why or why not? What kinds of things cause you to miss these special moments?

2. Which simple moments do you recall with joy? Which moments do you wish you could relive? Why?

3. Reread 1 Thessalonians 5:18. What does this verse mean? How can we do this, particularly when our circumstances are much less than perfect? Are there ways in which we can cultivate attitudes of thankfulness? Explain your answer.

4. As you think about your children, what are you most thankful for today?

5. Why don't more mothers talk about the importance of being thankful in all circumstances? When do you find it particularly hard to be thankful?

CHAPTER SEVENTEEN

1. When have you felt as if you had reached "the end"?

2. Reflecting on difficulties you have faced, which "beginnings" occurred when you had given up hope?

3. Why is it important for us to identify and face our disappointments? What happens if we "stuff" them and pretend that everything is okay?

4. Where does God fit into the picture when we experience deep pain? Why do bad things happen to good people?

CHAPTER EIGHTEEN

1. In what way(s) did you identify with the author's housecleaning challenges?

2. How do you feel when your mothering duties keep you from cleaning?

3. When things get cluttered, how does the "controlled chaos" affect you?

4. What have you learned so far about how to keep your home going *and* handle all your other responsibilities?

5. How have your expectations of what housekeeping would be like, while carrying a child, changed since you were first pregnant?

6. Do you agree that "having kids means sacrificing some tidiness"? Why or why not?

7. What benefits might there be in talking about practical housekeeping issues with other mothers?

8. What did you feel as you read the poem?

CHAPTER NINETEEN

1. Why are our words of appreciation so necessary for our children?

2. Do you find it easy to praise your children? Why or why not?

3. To what extent might our ability to give "nice words" reflect the words of praise we did or didn't receive as we were growing up? Is it possible to learn new ways

of using words even when we haven't had good models to learn from? Explain your answer.

4. What does a sincere "thank you" communicate to a child?

5. How do you tend to use words? As you speak with your children, do you find it easy or difficult to use positive words rather than words of criticism and judgment? Why is it important for each of us to evaluate the words we use with our children?

CHAPTER TWENTY

1. Why is forgiveness such a powerful force in relationships?

2. What emotions tend to develop when forgiveness is not granted?

3. How can we model what forgiveness is all about with our children? If you are discussing these questions in a group, talk about times when you needed to forgive and/or needed to ask for forgiveness.

4. Do you think it's possible for us to forgive as God forgives us? Why or why not?

CHAPTER TWENTY-ONE

1. What point do you think von Goethe emphasized in his quotation at the start of this chapter?

2. When stressful situations occur in your household, how do you tend to respond?

3. Where does the ability to be patient with our children come from? What can we do when we tend to exhibit more impatience than patience?

CHAPTER TWENTY-TWO

1. Reread the quotation by Lady Bird Johnson at the beginning of this chapter.

   • As you were growing up, what did people believe about you? How did those beliefs affect you—positively and/or negatively?

   • Why does what we believe about our children influence them so greatly?

2. Where do you get wise advice about parenting?

3. Which items in the "Don'ts" list connected with you? Why? What changes might you need to make in your parenting?

4. What did you feel as you read the "Dos" list? Which tips might you add to the list?

5. Why is it hard sometimes to ask for advice?

CHAPTER TWENTY-THREE

1. How do you tend to respond when people do things differently from how you would do them?

2. Why is it important to discover our gifts? To help other people discover their gifts?

3. When do you think it's good to delegate duties? How often do *you* delegate?

CHAPTER TWENTY-FOUR

1. Why do you think the author uses quotes that emphasize the importance of humor?

2. How might today be different if you focus on making at least three positive deposits in the memory bank(s) of your children?

3. As you were growing up, which occurred more frequently: laughter or harsh ridicule and blame? Why? How has what you experienced as a child influenced you, particularly in how you respond to your children?

4. Why can some people laugh about a family situation in which another family would become upset?

5. What are some ways in which we can break bad cycles of tension and interject humor and positive feedback instead?

6. If you don't laugh much, what can you do to learn more about a cheerful heart? (Reread Proverbs 17:22.)

CHAPTER TWENTY-FIVE

1. Do you agree with the quotation from Abraham Lincoln? Why or why not?

2. What point was the author making with the Sharky story?

3. Think about some of your family's favorite memories. What made them special?

4. Given your responsibilities, which things matter most to you as demonstrated by the amount of time you spend doing them?

5. What might you do this coming week to exhibit more sensitivity to other people's feelings?

CHAPTER TWENTY-SIX

1. Which holidays are special for your family? Why? If you are in a group setting, share a special memory.

2. Do you agree that the love in a home is far more important than how orderly everything is? Explain your answer.

3. Think about how God has blessed you. Which blessings are you particularly thankful for today?

4. Why do you think God wants us to thank him for what he has done for us? How can we cultivate a spirit of thankfulness?

CHAPTER TWENTY–SEVEN

1. Why is it important for us to screen the electronic media our children watch—television shows, movies, computer games, and so forth?

2. What standards do you use when selecting your children's entertainment?

3. Reread Philippians 4:8–9. How can we model these verses for our children? How can we teach them to think about the things in these verses?

4. What role do you think God wants to have in the decisions we make on behalf of our children?

CHAPTER TWENTY–EIGHT

1. What does Emerson's quotation at the beginning of this chapter mean?

2. Why do we sometimes hide parts of ourselves that could bring light into the lives of other people?

3. In what way(s) can you help your children share their "light" with other people? Encourage them to let their uniqueness shine forth?

4. What will you do this week to allow the light of Jesus' presence to shine through you toward other people?

CHAPTER TWENTY-NINE

1. What is involved in "trusting God"?

2. How can we teach our children to trust God?

3. Which parenting situation(s) causes you to feel the most stress?

4. What does 1 Peter 5:7 reveal? Why do we sometimes try to carry our worries ourselves instead of giving them to God?

5. This week, what will you do to teach your children about God's unfailing love and peace?

CHAPTER THIRTY

1. How much in control do you feel you have to be? Why? What do your children do that reminds you that you can't—and shouldn't try to—completely control their environments?

2. What worries you most about being a mother? About your children?

3. Why is prayer to be an important part of the mothering process?

4. How does what we believe about God affect our desire to spend time with him? To share our child-related concerns with him?

5. Think about a time when God revealed his love to you and/or your child? How did you feel afterward?

6. Reflect on where your hope lies. Is it in yourself and your abilities? In what you've learned? In relationships? As mentioned in Psalm 33:22, does it lie in God?

7. As you think about your life so far, what do you think God is trying to teach you about depending on him? About entrusting your children to him? What kinds of things sidetrack you from trusting God fully?

CHAPTER THIRTY-ONE

1. Why is it important to live life one moment and one day at a time? In our culture, what makes this difficult?

2. Which precious moments might you treasure today that you might otherwise overlook?

3. According to Psalm 33:21, why are we to rejoice?

4. Which three things will you do this coming week, based on ideas you've read in this book?

About the Author

Cheryl Kirking is a popular speaker, author, and songwriter who loves motherhood and knows the importance of finding the blessings in every day. She is a former high school teacher and concert artist, who now tickles the funny bones and tugs at the heart-strings of audiences nationwide, including at conferences for women, teachers, churches, and business organizations. She and her husband and triplets live in Wisconsin.

Cheryl's other books include
Ripples of Joy (Shaw/Waterbrook)
All Is Calm, All Is Bright (Baker Books)
Teacher, You're an A+ (Harvest House)

For information on having Cheryl Kirking speak at your event, call CLASS Speakers at 1-800-433-6633, or visit her Web site at www.cherylkirking.com.

The Word at Work Around the World

A vital part of Cook Communications Ministries is our international outreach, Cook Communications Ministries International (CCMI). Your purchase of this book, and of other books and Christian-growth products from Cook, enables CCMI to provide Bibles and Christian literature to people in more than 150 languages in 65 countries.

Cook Communications Ministries is a not-for-profit, self-supporting organization. Revenues from sales of our books, Bible curricula, and other church and home products not only fund our U.S. ministry, but also fund our CCMI ministry around the world. One hundred percent of donations to CCMI go to our international literature programs.

CCMI reaches out internationally in three ways:

· Our premier International Christian Publishing Institute (ICPI) trains leaders from nationally led publishing houses around the world.

· We provide literature for pastors, evangelists, and Christian workers in their national language.

· We reach people at risk—refugees, AIDS victims, street children, and famine victims—with God's Word.

Word Power, God's Power

Faith Kidz, RiverOak, Honor, Life Journey, Victor, NexGen — every time you purchase a book produced by Cook Communications Ministries, you not only meet a vital personal need in your life or in the life of someone you love, but you're also a part of ministering to José in Colombia, Humberto in Chile, Gousa in India, or Lidiane in Brazil. You help make it possible for a pastor in China, a child in Peru, or a mother in West Africa to enjoy a life-changing book. And because you helped, children and adults around the world are learning God's Word and walking in his ways.

Thank you for your partnership in helping to disciple the world. May God bless you with the power of his Word in your life.

For more information about our international ministries, visit www.ccmi.org.

Additional copies of *Crayons in the Dryer*
are available wherever good books are sold.

If you have enjoyed this book, or if it has had an impact on
your life, we would like to hear from you.

Please contact us at:

LIFE JOURNEY BOOKS
Cook Communications Ministries, Dept. 201
4050 Lee Vance View
Colorado Springs, CO 80918

Or visit our Web site: www.cookministries.com